Physics!
BEST
SCIENCE
PROJECTS

Light, Sound, and Waves Science Fair Projects

Using Sunglasses, Guitars, CDs, and Other Stuff

Robert Gardner

Enslow Publishers, Inc.

40 Industrial Road	PO Box 38
Box 398	Aldershot
Berkeley Heights, NJ 07922	Hants GU12 6BP
USA	UK

http://www.enslow.com

Library of Congress Cataloging-in-Publication Data

Gardner, Robert, 1929–
    Light, sound, and waves science fair projects using sunglasses, guitars, CDs, and other
stuff / Robert Gardner.
        v. cm. — (Physics! best science projects)
    Includes index.
    Contents: Some properties of sound and waves — Some properties of light — Light,
sound, and reflection — Light, sound, and refraction — Dispersion, light, and color —
Sound, light, and waves — Transverse waves and polarized light.
    ISBN 0-7660-2126-2 (hardcover)
    1. Light—Experiments—Juvenile literature. 2. Sound—Experiments—Juvenile
literature. 3. Wave-motion, Theory of—Experiments—Juvenile literature. [1. Light—
Experiments. 2. Sound—Experiments. 3. Waves—Experiments. 4. Experiments.]
    I. Title. II. Series.
    QC360.G373 2004
    507'.8—dc22
                                                    2003013713

Printed in the United States of America

10 9 8 7 6 5 4

To Our Readers: We have done our best to make sure all Internet Addresses in this
book were active and appropriate when we went to press. However, the author and the
publisher have no control over and assume no liability for the material available on those
Internet sites or on other Web sites they may link to. Any comments or suggestions can
be sent by e-mail to comments@enslow.com or to the address on the back cover.

Illustration Credits: All illustrations by Tom LaBaff, except: pp. 61, 71, 74, 104,
105, 114 by Enslow Publishers, Inc.; pp. 22, 29, 89, 91, 94 by Stephen F. Delisle.

Cover Photo: Hemera Technologies, Inc. 1997–2000.

Contents

Introduction

Physics is the part of science that deals with matter and energy. You and the world around you are made up of matter. All activity involves energy. Some activities produce light or sound or both. By understanding physics, you can unlock the secrets of matter and energy.

By doing the experiments in this book, you will discover the wave nature of sound and light (as it is understood so far) and how sound and light travel through space. You will come to understand how the drummer in your favorite band produces deep bass sounds and why you and your friends look so weird in fun-house mirrors.

Most of the materials you will need to carry out these activities can be found in your home. Several of the experiments may require inexpensive items that you can buy in a supermarket, a hobby or toy shop, a hardware store, or from one of the science suppliers listed in the appendix. Some may call for articles that you may be able to borrow from your school's science department. Occasionally, you will need someone to work with you on an experiment that requires a subject or a helper. It would be best if you work with friends or adults who enjoy experimenting as much as you do. That way everyone will enjoy what you are doing. **If any danger is involved in doing an experiment, it will be made known to you. In some cases, to avoid any danger to you, you will be**

asked to work with an adult. Please do so. Do not take any chances that could lead to an injury.

Like any good scientist, you will find it useful to record your ideas, notes, data, and anything you can conclude from your experiments in a notebook. By so doing, you can keep track of the information you gather and the conclusions you reach. It will allow you to refer to experiments you have done and help you with other projects in the future.

SCIENCE FAIRS

Many of the experiments in this book are followed by sections called Science Project Ideas. These ideas may be the start of a science fair project. However, judges at such fairs do not reward projects or experiments that are simply copied from a book. For example, a diagram or model of a incandescent light-bulb would not impress judges; however, a unique method for measuring the wavelength of light or sound would gain serious consideration.

Science fair judges tend to reward creative thought and imagination. It is difficult to be creative or imaginative unless you are really interested in your project. Be sure to choose a subject that appeals to you. And before you jump into a project, consider, too, your own talents and the cost of materials you will need.

If you decide to use a project found in this book for a science fair, you should find ways to take a fresh approach or extend the project. As you do these projects, new ideas for experiments will probably come into your mind. Experiments that are your own ideas and are interesting to you could make excellent science fair projects.

If you decide to enter a science fair and have never done so before, you should read some of the books listed in the Further Reading section. Some of these books deal specifically with science fairs and will provide plenty of helpful hints and lots of useful information that will enable you to avoid the pitfalls that sometimes plague first-time entrants. You will learn how to prepare appealing reports that include charts and graphs, how to set up and display your work, how to present your project, and how to relate to judges and visitors.

SAFETY FIRST

Most of the projects included in this book are perfectly safe. However, the following safety rules are well worth reading before you start any project.

- ✓ Do any experiments or projects, whether from this book or of your own design, under the supervision of a science teacher or other knowledgeable adult.

- ✓ Read all instructions carefully before proceeding with a project. If you have questions, check with your supervisor before going any further.

✓ Maintain a serious attitude while conducting experiments. Fooling around can be dangerous to you and to others.

✓ Wear approved safety goggles when you are working with a flame or doing anything that might cause injury to your eyes.

✓ Do not eat or drink while experimenting.

✓ Have a first-aid kit nearby while you are experimenting.

✓ Do not put your fingers or any object other than properly designed electrical connectors into electrical outlets.

✓ Never let water droplets come in contact with a hot lightbulb.

✓ Never experiment with household electricity except under the supervision of a knowledgeable adult.

✓ The liquid in some thermometers is mercury. It is dangerous to touch mercury or to breathe mercury vapor, and such thermometers have been banned in many states. When doing these experiments, use only non-mercury thermometers, such as those filled with alcohol. If you have a mercury thermometer in the house, **ask an adult** if it can be taken to a local mercury thermometer exchange location.

Chapter 1

Some Properties of Sound and Waves

Stop, close your eyes, and listen. How many different sounds do you hear? Did you know that all sounds are caused by vibrations (something moving back and forth)? If you listen to loud music, you know that sounds can be felt as well as heard.

Human ears can detect a vibration repeated 20 to 20,000 times per second. The number of vibrations per second is called a frequency. Frequencies are measured in hertz (Hz). A frequency of 20 vibrations per second is 20 Hz.

Dogs can hear much higher frequencies than humans. Some high-frequency whistles used to call dogs cannot be heard by humans. Bats and dolphins emit sounds with frequencies as high as 100,000 Hz. They use such sounds to detect small objects. We use sonar and radar for the same purpose, but animals' "radar" is built-in.

In this chapter, you will investigate the sources of sounds and how sounds travel. You will also discover how to measure sound intensities, and see how waves can serve as a model for the transmission of sound.

Experiment 1.1

The Source of Sounds

Materials

- ✓ flexible ruler or hacksaw blade
- ✓ table
- ✓ guitar or other stringed instrument
- ✓ lids of cooking pots
- ✓ clean table fork
- ✓ sink
- ✓ rubber band
- ✓ shoe box
- ✓ shoe
- ✓ tuning fork

(You may be able to borrow some of these items from your school's science or music departments.)

Because a flexible ruler or hacksaw blade will vibrate, it can be used to produce sound. Hold half of the ruler or blade firmly against a tabletop. Let the other half project beyond the table, as shown in Figure 1. Use a finger to pluck the end of the ruler that is free to move. What do you hear?

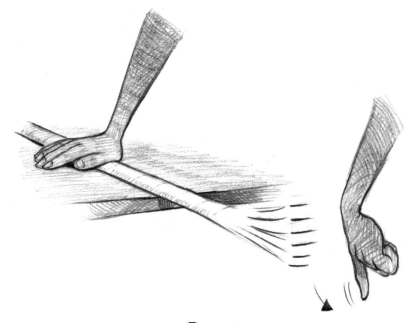

Figure 1.

To see that vibrations produce sounds, just pluck the end of a flexible ruler or hacksaw blade.

Pitch is the word used for how high or low a tone is. What happens to the pitch of the sound if you reduce the length that is free to vibrate? What happens to the sound's pitch if you increase the length that is free to vibrate?

If possible, pluck the string of a guitar or other stringed instrument to make it vibrate. Listen to the sound made by the vibrating string. What can you do to change the pitch of the sound it makes?

Hold the lid of a cooking pot by its handle and strike it with the tines of a clean table fork. Listen to the sound the vibrating lid makes. Does the size of the lid affect the sound it makes?

Do you think the fork tines are also vibrating? To find out, strike the lid with the fork again. Then hold the fork next to one ear. Are the fork's tines vibrating? How does the sound they make compare with the sound from the lid? Which makes a louder sound? Which produces a higher-pitched sound?

Strike the fork tines against a sink and listen to the sound they make. Strike it again, and hold the handle of the fork between your teeth. How does the loudness of this sound compare with the previous one?

Your teeth are fixed in your jawbone. Your jaw is connected to the bones of your skull. Your inner ear, where sound is converted to nerve impulses, is located deep inside your skull. Based on this experiment, is air or bone the better conductor of sound?

Stretch a rubber band and pluck it. Note the amplitude (loudness) of the sound it makes. Next, place the rubber band around an empty open shoe box. What do you notice about the amplitude of the sound when you again pluck the rubber band? What happens to the pitch of the sound when you stretch the rubber band some more and then pluck it?

Tap a tuning fork against your shoe and then hold it near your ear. Describe the pitch of the sound. If it is a middle-C tuning fork, its frequency of vibration is 256 Hz. That means it vibrates 256 times in one second. Strike the tuning fork again and hold its base against a tabletop. What happens to the amplitude of the sound when you do this? If you touch the table, can you feel the vibrations?

Science Project Ideas

- Design a demonstration to show why guitars, violins, and other stringed instruments have a hollow wooden box beneath the strings.

- Use a tape recorder to record a variety of sounds. You might record a squeaky door, a dog drinking water, leaves rustling, an automobile engine, rain falling on a roof, and so on. How many of these sounds can various people identify?

Experiment 1.2

Air Pulses, Sounds, and Waves

Materials

- ✓ **an adult**
- ✓ drill and bit (0.6 to 1.2 cm or ¼ to ½ in)
- ✓ empty coffee can with plastic lid
- ✓ candle and candleholder
- ✓ matches
- ✓ one-gallon plastic milk container
- ✓ yardstick
- ✓ 6 marbles
- ✓ grooved ruler

As you saw in the previous experiment, sound can travel through air. Unlike light, it cannot travel through empty space. A source of sound, such as a bell, cannot be heard if it is placed in a vacuum, a space from which air has been removed.

When something vibrates, it pushes on the air around it. To see that a simple signal can travel through air, **ask an adult** to drill a hole about 0.6 to 1.2 cm (¼ to ½ in) in diameter in the bottom of an empty coffee can. Put the plastic lid on the top of the can. Place the bottom of the can near your face. Hit the center of the lid with your knuckles. Do you feel a pulse of air hit your face?

Put a candle in a candleholder and place it on a table. **Under adult supervision,** light the candle. Hold the coffee can near the flame and aim the hole at the flame. Again, make an air pulse by striking the lid. Did the flame flutter when the air pulse reached it? Can you put out the flame by making air pulses with the coffee can?

Can you do better with an empty one-gallon plastic milk container? Aim the mouth of the container toward the flame. Then hit the bottom of the container with your fist. Did you put out the flame? What is the greatest distance that you can hold the empty milk container from the candle and still put out the flame?

With practice, you will find that you can use the milk container to blow out a candle flame from distances of 1.5 to 2 meters (5 to 6 feet).

You have seen that a pulse of air can travel from its origin to points quite far away. The vibrations that cause sound can produce similar pulses that travel through air to your ear. Air, like all gases, is made up of tiny particles called molecules. Find about half a dozen identical marbles to represent air molecules. Put the marbles about a centimeter apart on a grooved ruler, as shown in Figure 2. Roll another marble, representing an air molecule that has been pushed by a vibrating object, into the marbles on the ruler. When the moving marble strikes the marble nearest to it, the marbles bump into one another in turn.

This successive bumping of one marble into another is a model for molecular bumping that transmits a pulse through the air. In the regions where molecules are colliding, the concentration of molecules is greater. The higher concentration of molecules causes an increase in air pressure. The successive

Figure 2.

Marbles can be used to represent molecules of air. What happens when one molecule bumps into another?

bumping results in a pulse of air pressure that travels through the air. In the case of sound, which results from vibrations, a series of pulses is produced. The sequence of pulses is called a sound wave.

The human eardrum is incredibly sensitive to changes in air pressure. It can detect intensities as small as a trillionth of a watt per square meter—less power per area than is needed to flutter a leaf on a tree.

Science Project Idea

- Design an experiment to show that sound does not move through a vacuum.

Experiment 1.3

Conduction of Sound

Materials

- ✓ watch or a small alarm clock that makes a ticking sound
- ✓ wooden table
- ✓ drinking glass
- ✓ small box, such as a shoe box
- ✓ newspaper
- ✓ packing materials such as chips, towels, and aluminum foil

You know that air can conduct (carry) sound. Will other kinds of matter conduct sound?

To find out, you will need a watch or a small alarm clock that makes a ticking sound. Place the face of the timepiece on a wooden table. Place your ear at the end of the table. Can you hear the ticking sound through the air? Move the timepiece to a point on the table where you can just barely hear it. Then place your ear firmly against the table, as shown in Figure 3a. Can you hear the ticking sound? If you can, is it louder or softer than it was when you heard it through air? Is wood or air the better conductor of sound?

Hold one side of a drinking glass firmly against your ear (Figure 3b). Hold a ticking timepiece against the other side of the glass. Can you hear the ticking sound?

a)

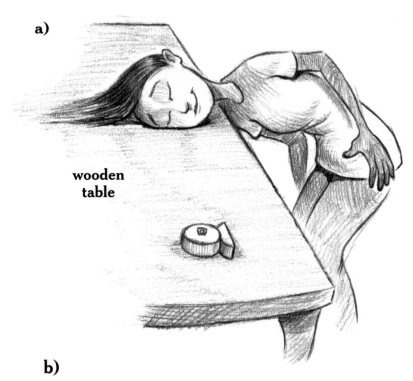

wooden table

b)

Figure 3.

a) Is wood or air the better conductor of sound?

b) Is air or glass the better conductor of sound?

Remove the glass without moving the timepiece. Can you still hear the ticking? If you can, is it louder or softer than it was with the glass in place? Is glass or air the better conductor of sound?

Put the ticking timepiece in a small box. Put your ear against the side of the box. You should be able to hear the ticking sound. Now, surround the timepiece and fill the box with crumpled newspaper. Can you still hear the timepiece? What can you say about the conduction of sound through crumpled newspaper?

Repeat the experiment several times using packing chips, towels, and crumpled aluminum foil in place of the crumpled newspaper. Which materials are poor sound conductors? Which, if any, are good conductors of sound?

Science Project Ideas

- Design and carry out experiments to compare the conduction of sound through water and metals with its conduction through air.

- Design and carry out experiments to compare the conduction of sound through different gases.

- Investigate why foghorns emit only low-pitched sounds.

- Why does a recording of your voice not sound like the voice you hear when you speak?

Experiment 1.4

Sound and Energy

Materials

- ✓ large bowl
- ✓ plastic wrap
- ✓ table salt
- ✓ wooden or plastic cooking spoon
- ✓ cooking pan

Energy comes in many forms, but one form is motion. Any moving object has what is known as kinetic energy. An object can be made to move by doing work on it—that is, by transferring energy to it. Your eardrum is sensitive to sound because sound is a form of energy. Sounds can make your eardrums move with each succeeding air pulse that strikes them. To see that sounds can make an eardrum move, make a membrane by covering a large bowl with plastic wrap. Be sure the plastic is stretched tightly so that it is taut like the cover on a drum.

Sprinkle some salt crystals onto the plastic wrap. Gently tap the plastic membrane with your finger. What happens to the salt crystals?

Now make a sound by clapping your hands near the bowl. What happens to the salt crystals?

Next, use a wooden or plastic cooking spoon to strike the bottom of a metal cooking pan near the bowl. What happens to the salt crystals? Can you make the salt crystals move by singing a note near the bowl? Does the pitch of the note you sing make a difference in the way the crystals move?

Experiment 1.5

Waves: A Model for Sound

Materials

- ✓ long Slinky or several short Slinkies tied together with twisties
- ✓ long, smooth floor
- ✓ a partner
- ✓ piece of yarn

Sound and air pulses cannot be seen, but you can feel pulses of air and hear and feel sound. You can use a Slinky to see how sound waves (successive pulses of air pressure) travel through air.

Place the Slinky on a long, smooth floor, such as a hallway. Have a partner hold one end of the Slinky firmly in place while you hold the other end. To make a pulse in the Slinky, push your end of the Slinky forward (toward your partner) quickly and then pull it back. Watch the pulse of compressed coils move along the Slinky to your partner. Is the pulse reflected (sent back) after it reaches your partner's fixed hand? Is sound ever reflected? (Think about echoes!)

Your push on the Slinky corresponds to the push air molecules receive when you make a pulse of air. Sounds involve successive pulses generated by a vibrating object. To make multiple pulses on the Slinky, move your end of the Slinky forward and back in rhythmic fashion. Your partner must hold the other end firmly in place. Watch a series of pulses move along the Slinky to the other end. Then stop producing pulses, but watch the last few you generated. Are they reflected when they reach your partner?

A series of evenly spaced pulses forms a longitudinal wave, one along the length, as shown in Figure 4. The places where the Slinky coils are close together are called compressions. They represent molecules of air pushed together by a vibrating object. The places where the coils are farther apart are called rarefactions. They correspond to regions of low air pressure where the molecules are less concentrated. A rarefaction is made by a vibrating object as it swings back after having pushed molecules together. As it swings back, it leaves a space where molecules are less concentrated (or rarer, in a way).

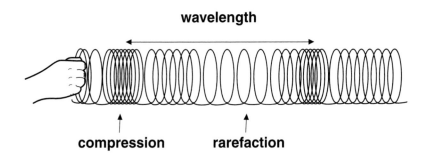

Figure 4.

A longitudinal wave on a Slinky. The wave on the Slinky is similar to a sound wave moving through air.

Like sound waves, the waves on the Slinky are longitudinal waves. They move up and down the length of the Slinky by the forward and backward movement of the coils that make up the Slinky. The distance between one compression and the next is a wavelength. The number of waves produced in one second is the frequency of the waves.

The Slinky is only a one-dimensional model. Actual sound waves, unless blocked, spread out in all directions. It is important to understand that while longitudinal waves move along a Slinky or through the air, the Slinky's coils or the molecules of air simply move back and forth. They transport the waves, but they do not move with them. To see that this is true, tie a piece of yarn to one coil of the Slinky. The yarn does not move along the Slinky, it simply moves back and forth. You have probably seen sports fans do the wave at stadium games. People simply stand and then sit while the wave moves around the stadium.

Science Project Ideas

- Show that the speed at which a wave moves is equal to its wavelength times its frequency.

- What is the Doppler effect and how is it related to sound waves?

Experiment 1.6

Another Kind of Wave

Materials

- ✓ long Slinky
- ✓ 2 partners
- ✓ clamps
- ✓ stringed instrument, such as a guitar, banjo, or violin
- ✓ 2 lengths of rubber tubing about 5 m (16 ft) long
- ✓ water
- ✓ pail or sink

The waves you saw moving along the Slinky in Experiment 1.5 were longitudinal waves. Each pulse as it travels along the Slinky moves parallel to the Slinky (forward and backward). But you can make waves that move perpendicular to the Slinky (up and down) as they travel along the Slinky. These are called transverse waves. To make a transverse pulse, move your end of the Slinky to the side and then back again in one very quick motion. You can watch this transverse pulse, like the one shown in Figure 5a, travel to the other end of the Slinky held by your partner. Does the pulse come back toward you? How can you make transverse waves like those in Figure 5b?

To see another example of transverse waves, use a stringed instrument, such as a guitar, banjo, or violin. Pluck one of the strings. Notice how the string vibrates in a direction perpendicular to the string itself.

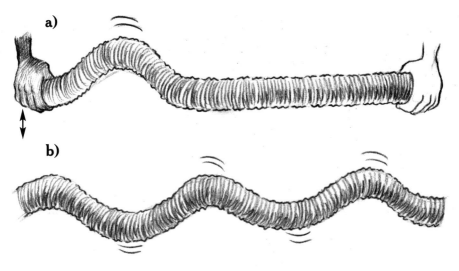

a)

b)

Figure 5.

a) You can make a transverse wave on a Slinky by quickly moving the end of the Slinky to the side and back again.

b) Can you make transverse waves like the ones shown here?

You can also make a transverse pulse on a rubber tube. Find a length of rubber tubing about 5 meters (16 feet) long. Have a partner hold one end while you hold the other end. Pull the tubing so that it is tight and under some tension. Use the side of your free hand to strike the tubing sharply near your end. Watch the pulse travel along the tubing.

To see how tension affects the speed at which the waves travel, you will need another piece of rubber tubing identical to the first. Hold the ends of both tubes, one in each hand. Have two partners hold the other ends of the tubes. Have one partner stretch one length of tubing so that it is under more tension than the tubing held by the other partner. Send pulses along the two tubes at the same time. How does the speed of the pulse on the two tubes compare? What effect does tension have on the speed at which waves travel along the rubber tubing? How can you increase the speed at which waves travel along the tubing?

Will the speed at which waves travel along a tube be affected by the weight of the tube? To find out, fill one of the tubes with water by lowering it into a water-filled pail or sink. Clamp both ends of the tube so that the water cannot spill out. Compare the speed at which transverse pulses travel along the empty tube and the water-filled tube. How does weight affect the speed at which waves move along a rubber tube?

Science Project Ideas

- Design and carry out experiments to find out if tension and weight affect the speed of transverse and longitudinal waves on a Slinky.

- Design and carry out experiments to find out how tension and weight affect the frequency of vibration (pitch) of strings. You might find fishing lines of different thickness useful for these experiments. If you do not play a stringed instrument, ask someone who does to show you how tension and weight affect a string's frequency (pitch).

Experiment 1.7

Converting Longitudinal Waves to Transverse Waves

Materials

✓ felt-tipped pen
✓ yardstick
✓ table

✓ a partner
✓ sheet of white paper

Although sound waves are longitudinal, they are often represented by transverse waves because transverse waves are easier to draw. To see one way that this can be done, tape a felt-tipped pen to the end of a yardstick as shown in Figure 6. Place the yardstick on a table. About half the yardstick should project beyond the edge of the table. Have a partner hold the yardstick firmly against the table, while you pluck the extended end that is free to vibrate. You will hear the sound waves made by the vibrating yardstick. Hold one edge of a sheet of white paper gently against the tip of the oscillating pen. Move the paper horizontally. The pen will leave a wave pattern on the paper. Be sure you do not press the paper too hard against the pen's tip or it will quickly stop the yardstick's motion. What kind of wave pattern do you see on the paper? Examine the pattern. You will see that the amplitude (Figure 7) of the wave decreases over time. Can you explain why?

Figure 6.

Tape a pen to a yardstick. Make the yardstick vibrate. Move a piece of paper horizontally so that the pen marks the paper as the yardstick moves up and down.

Next, move the yardstick so that only about 30 cm (12 in) projects beyond the table. Repeat the experiment. How do the sounds made by the vibrating yardstick compare when it was shorter and longer? If you move the paper at the same speed as before, you will see that the wavelength is shorter. Can you explain why?

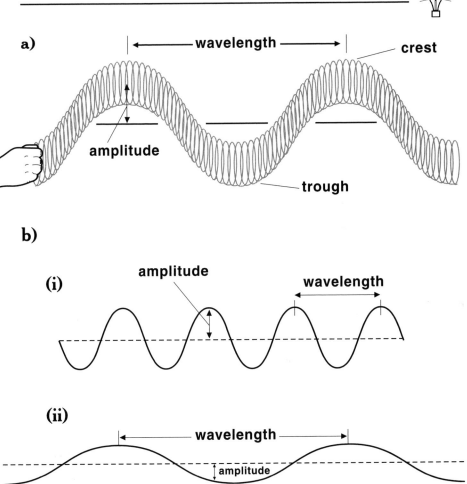

Figure 7.

a) The highest point of a transverse wave is called a crest. The lowest is called a trough. The distance between successive crests or troughs is one wavelength. The amplitude of a wave is the amount that a crest or trough is displaced from its normal rest position.

b) Examples of transverse waves are shown here. Wave *i* has a shorter wavelength and a larger amplitude than wave *ii*.

Intensity of Sound: Loudness

Materials

- ✓ sound-level meter (from school or electronics store)
- ✓ ear-protecting gear
- ✓ a variety of places
- ✓ CD player
- ✓ yardstick

The human ear can detect sounds with intensities as small as a trillionth of a watt per square meter (W/m^2). The scale used to measure the intensity of sound has its zero value at the lower threshold (limit) of hearing. Sound intensity, commonly known as loudness, is measured in bels (B), named in honor of Alexander Graham Bell, who invented the telephone. More commonly, scientists use the decibel (dB), which is one tenth of a bel. When the intensity of a sound, as measured in W/m^2, increases by ten times, the measurement in bels increases by 10 dB or 1 B.

Table 1 gives the intensity of various common sounds.

Use a sound-level meter to measure the intensity of sound in different places. **Wear ear-protecting gear while testing near noisy places.** You might try some of the sound sources listed in Table 1, as well as a busy classroom, a classroom during a test, a playground, a baseball or football stadium after the home team scores and after the visiting team scores, your house at night and at breakfast, and other noisy and quiet areas.

Table 1.

INTENSITIES OF DIFFERENT SOUNDS IN BELS, DECIBELS, WATTS PER SQUARE METER, AND COMPARED TO THE THRESHOLDS OF HEARING AND EAR PAIN

Source of sound	Intensity of sound in B	Intensity of sound in dB	Intensity of sound in W/m²	Intensity relative to threshold of hearing
threshold of hearing	0	0	1 trillionth	1
rustling leaves	1	10	10 trillionths	10 times
whispering	2	20	100 trillionths	100 times
normal conversation	4	40	10 billionths	10,000 times
vacuum cleaner	7	70	10 millionths	10 million times
heavy traffic	9	90	1 thousandth	1 billion times
riveter at work	10	100	1 hundredth	10 billion times
loud rock music	12	120	1	1 trillion times
threshold of ear pain	12	120	1	1 trillion times
jet airplane	15	150	1,000	1 quadrillion times
rocket engine	18	180	1 million	1 quintillion times

How does the distance from the sound source affect the intensity of sound? To find out, measure the loudest sound from a small battery-powered CD player or boom box. To avoid reflected sounds, do this experiment outside. Hold the meter several yards from the sound and record the loudest sound indicated by the meter. What happens to the sound intensity when you double the distance from the sound source? Remember, a decrease of 10 dB means the intensity is one-tenth as great. A decrease of 3 dB indicates the intensity has just about halved. What do you find when you triple the distance?

Chapter 2

Some Properties of Light

In Chapter 1 you saw that sound is produced when something vibrates. The source of light is not as easy to discover. We can all name sources of light: incandescent bulbs; fluorescent bulbs; the sun and other stars; flames from burning candles, logs, and various fuels; neon signs; and so on. But how do stars, bulbs, candles, and other things produce light? In the 1870s, James Clerk Maxwell, a Scots physicist, developed mathematical equations to show that, for all sources of light, the light actually comes from moving electrical charges. In fact, Maxwell showed that visible light is just a small part of the electromagnetic spectrum, a spectrum that extends from gamma rays to radio waves. And, like sound, light is a form of energy. You can convince yourself that light is energy by doing Experiment 2.1.

Experiment 2.1

Light and Energy

Materials

- ✓ radiometer (from school, hobby store, or science supply company)
- ✓ lightbulb and socket
- ✓ sheet of cardboard
- ✓ black cloth
- ✓ alcohol-based thermometer

Examine a radiometer like the one shown in Figure 8. The radiometer consists of a transparent globe from which most of the air has been removed. As a result, the vanes, which can turn on a needlelike point, are in a space that is nearly a vacuum. Notice that each vane on the radiometer has a dark side and a bright side. Radiometers measure the intensity of radiant energy.

Place the radiometer near a lightbulb. What happens inside the radiometer when light shines on the vanes? What happens if you place a sheet of cardboard between the light and the radiometer? What evidence do you have that light is a form of energy? How do you think the energy is transferred to the radiometer?

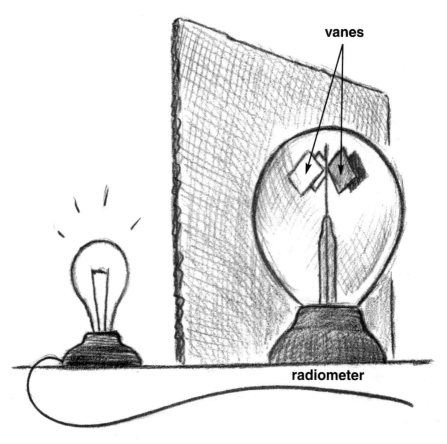

Figure 8.

What happens to the vanes of a radiometer when light shines on them?

Wrap a black cloth around the bulb end of an alcohol-based thermometer. Place the cloth-covered thermometer in bright sunlight. What happens to the temperature inside the cloth? What additional evidence do you now have to show that light is a form of energy?

Science Project Idea

● Find a way to make a radiometer run backwards; that is, turn with the shiny side trailing.

Experiment 2.2

The Path of Light

Materials

✓ paper punch

✓ 3 index cards (3 in × 5 in)

✓ 3 small wooden blocks

✓ tape

✓ meterstick or yardstick

✓ window

✓ a partner

✓ flashlight

✓ sheet of paper

✓ string, 2 meters (2 yards) long

Use a paper punch to make holes in three index cards at the same time. By holding the cards so that they are aligned, all the holes will be in the same position on the cards. Use tape to fasten the cards to three wooden blocks, as shown in Figure 9. Be sure the bottom edge of each card touches the bottom edge of each block. Place the cards about 50 cm (20 in) apart near a window. Look through the hole in one card. Move the second

Figure 9.

What must be true about light if you can see the same light through all three holes when the holes lie along a straight line?

card so that the light from the window passes through it as well as the card you are looking through. Finally, ask a partner to move the third card until you can see light from the window through all three holes.

To reach your eye, light from the window must pass through all three holes. Darken the room and hold a flashlight in front of the hole in the first card. Can you see a circle of light on a piece of paper your partner holds beyond the third hole?

Cut a piece of string about 2 meters (2 yards) long. Being careful not to move the cards, thread the string through all three holes. Have your partner hold one end of the string while you hold the other. Carefully tighten the string. Do the holes lie along a straight line? What does this tell you about the path followed by light?

Have you ever watched a carpenter as he looks down a board? What assumption is he making about the path followed by light?

Experiment 2.3

Straight Light Paths and Images

Materials

- ✓ **an adult**
- ✓ matches
- ✓ candle
- ✓ table or counter
- ✓ cardboard box
- ✓ ruler
- ✓ knife
- ✓ tape
- ✓ black construction paper

- ✓ large pin, such as a T-pin or hat pin
- ✓ sheet of white paper
- ✓ sheet of cardboard
- ✓ dark room
- ✓ clear lightbulb with a straight-line filament
- ✓ pencil

Here is another way to test the idea that light travels in straight lines. Figure 10a shows light rays (very narrow beams of light) coming from a bright object. If the rays pass through a tiny hole, they should form an upside-down image of the object on the screen on the opposite side of the hole. In this experiment, you will check to see if such an image can be produced. If it can, it offers more evidence that light travels in straight lines. As you can see from the drawing, when the screen and object are the same distance from the pinhole, the image will be the same size as the object.

Ask an adult to light a candle and put it on a table or counter. Place a box in front of the candle, as shown in Figure 10b. Cut a square hole in the box. Make the square about 2.5 cm (1 in) on a side. The hole should be about the same height above the table as the candle flame. Tape a piece of black construction paper over the hole. With a large pin, such as a T-pin or hat pin, make a small hole in the black paper.

Turn out all the lights so that the room is very dark except for the light from the candle flame. Hold a sheet of white paper taped to cardboard near the pinhole as shown. Can you find an image of the candle flame on the white paper? Is the image upside down? What happens to the size of the image as you move the white-paper screen closer to the pinhole? What happens to the size of the image when you move the screen farther from the pinhole? Using Figure 10a, see if you can explain why the size of the image changes as you move the screen closer to or farther from the pinhole.

Replace the candle with a clear lightbulb that has a straight-line filament. Turn the bulb so that the full length of its filament faces the pinhole. Does an image form when light from the lightbulb's filament passes through the pinhole?

a)

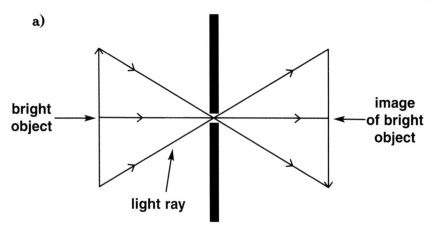

b)

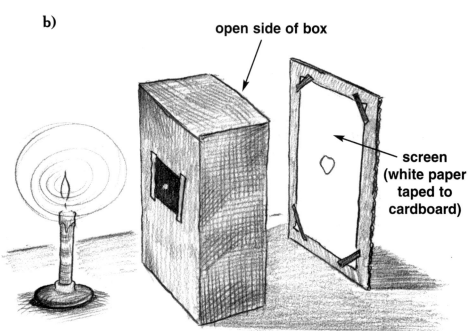

Figure 10.

a) When light rays from a bright object go through a small hole, an image will form on a screen.

b) A candle flame will form such a pinhole image.

Can you tell whether the image of the filament is reversed or upside down (inverted)? If not, slowly move a pencil across the front of the bulb as you watch the image. How does this help you to decide whether or not the image is reversed or inverted? Is the image reversed vertically? Is it reversed horizontally?

Place the screen and *filament* (not the outside of the bulb) so that they are both the same distance from the pinhole. Does the length of the image appear to be about the same as the length of the filament? What would you have to do to test this more closely?

Science Project Ideas

- On a bright, sunny day, look at the circles of light (sun dapples) that appear in the shade of a leafy tree. What do you think causes these circles? What experiment could you do to help confirm your explanation (hypothesis)?

- You can build a pinhole camera, which uses a pinhole in place of a lens. Such a camera can take photographs of stationary objects even in dim light. Why can't such a camera be used for action photos that require a short exposure?

Experiment 2.4

Shadows: More Evidence for Straight Light Paths

Materials

- ✓ dark room
- ✓ clear lightbulb with a straight-line filament
- ✓ frosted bulb
- ✓ meterstick or yardstick
- ✓ cardboard square, 10 cm (4 in) on a side
- ✓ a partner

In a dark room, turn on a clear lightbulb with a straight-line filament like the one you used in Experiment 2.3. Turn the bulb so that the end of its filament appears to be a point of light when seen from a white wall several meters (yards) away.

Hold your hand between the lightbulb and the wall. Describe the shadow of your hand on the wall. What happens to the size of the shadow as you move your hand closer to the wall? As you move it farther from the wall?

Where should you hold your hand to make the biggest shadow of your hand on the wall? Where should you hold your hand to make the smallest shadow of your hand on the wall? Can you make your hand's shadow smaller than your hand?

For a more quantitative look at shadows, place the point of light exactly 2 meters (6.5 ft) from the wall. Then place a square piece of cardboard 10 cm (4 in) on a side midway between the light and the wall, as shown in Figure 11. Ask a partner to measure the size of the shadow on the wall. Compare the lengths and widths of the shadow and the cardboard square. How do their areas compare?

Predict the size and area of the shadow when you hold the cardboard square 50 cm (20 in) from the light and when you

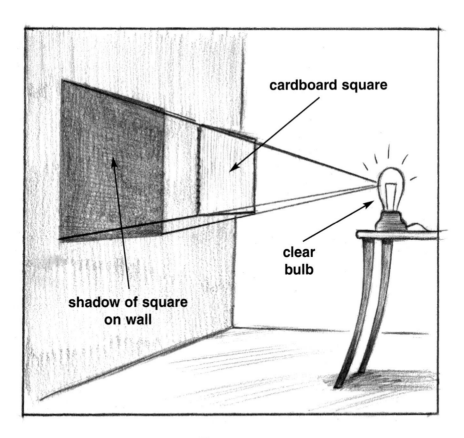

cardboard square

clear
bulb

shadow of square
on wall

Figure 11.

A cardboard square is held halfway between a point of light and a white wall. How large will the shadow of the square be?

hold it 50 cm (20 in) from the wall. Then test your predictions. Were you right? How do these shadows and their sizes provide evidence that light travels in straight lines?

Replace the clear bulb with a frosted bulb. Again, cast a shadow of your hand on the wall. Notice how the shadow becomes fuzzy when you hold your hand close to the bulb. Where can you hold your hand so as to make a sharper shadow similar to those you cast using the point of light? Why do you think shadows cast by the frosted bulb are fuzzier than those made using a point of light?

Science Project Ideas

- Using the clear bulb and the wall you used in Experiment 2.4, hold a metal can between the light and the wall. Turn the can in various ways. How many different shadow shapes can you make? Try some other objects such as a cone, a wooden block, an egg, a football, a basketball, and so on. What interesting shadow shapes can you make with them? Are there any objects for which the shadow shape does not change?

- Under what conditions will you or any object cast more than one shadow?

Experiment 2.5

Light Transmitters and Blockers

Materials

✓ glass	✓ colored plastic
✓ cardboard	✓ plastic wrap
✓ water	✓ tissue paper
✓ waxed paper	✓ mirror
✓ aluminum foil	✓ other materials

Some materials transmit light: They allow light to pass through. They are said to be transparent. Other materials block light by reflecting it, absorbing it, or both. They cast dark shadows and are said to be opaque. Translucent materials allow some light to pass, but they also scatter and absorb some. Objects cannot be seen clearly through translucent materials.

Test the following materials and classify them as transparent, opaque, or translucent: glass, cardboard, water, waxed paper, aluminum foil, colored plastic, plastic wrap, tissue paper, a mirror, your eyelids, and other available materials.

Experiment 2.6

Light Intensity (Brightness) and Distance

Materials

✓ **an adult**

✓ darkened room

✓ 2 square sheets of cardboard, about 60 cm (24 in) on a side

✓ point source of light, such as a clear bulb with a straight-line filament

✓ knife

✓ ruler

✓ meterstick or yardstick

✓ 2 strips of wood, about 60 cm (24 in) long, or about 4 thick books

✓ support to raise light

✓ a partner

If you did Experiment 1.8, you found that the intensity of a sound, measured in decibels, decreases significantly as you move farther from the sound. Does light behave in the same way?

The intensity of light (brightness) is the amount of light per unit area. To see how the intensity of light varies with distance, you will need a darkened room, two large sheets of cardboard, and a point of light. You can obtain a point of light by using a clear bulb with a straight-line filament like the one shown in Figure 12. Either end of the filament is a point of light. **Ask an adult** to use a knife to cut out a square 10 cm (4 in) on a side from the middle of one sheet of cardboard. On the second sheet of cardboard, draw a square 50 cm (20 in) on a side. Use a meterstick or yardstick to divide the large square into 25 squares, all 10 cm (4 in) on a side, as shown in Figure 12.

Now, turn on the light. Place the cardboard sheet with the hole in it upright and 25 cm (10 in) in front of the point of light, as shown in Figure 12. You can support it with some pieces of wood or books. This sheet of cardboard is not to be moved. You may have to raise the light to make it level with the hole in the cardboard. Next, ask a partner to hold the second sheet of cardboard upright and against the cardboard with the hole in it. Ask the partner to slowly move the second sheet away

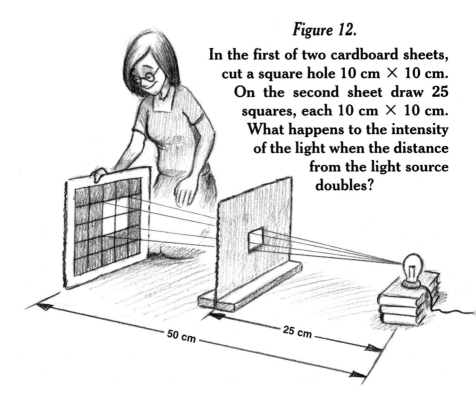

Figure 12.

In the first of two cardboard sheets, cut a square hole 10 cm × 10 cm. On the second sheet draw 25 squares, each 10 cm × 10 cm. What happens to the intensity of the light when the distance from the light source doubles?

50 cm

25 cm

from the hole until it is 50 cm (20 in) from the point of light, as shown. How many squares does the light that comes through the 10-cm-square hole cover on the second sheet of cardboard?

The area covered by the light coming through the 10-cm square is 10 cm ×10 cm, which is 100 square centimeters (100 cm^2) or 16 in^2. What area does that same light cover on the second sheet of cardboard? What has doubling the distance from 25 cm to 50 cm done to the area covered by the light? What has doubling the distance done to the intensity of the light?

Predict and then measure the area covered by the light shining on the second cardboard sheet when it is moved to 75 cm (30 in) from the point of light. What area will the light cover when the second sheet is placed 100 cm (40 in) from the point of light?

Science Project Idea

● Use a light meter to measure what happens to the intensity of a light source when the distance from the light is doubled. When it is tripled. When it is quadrupled.

Chapter 3

Light, Sound, and Reflection

When you look in a mirror, you see an image of yourself. Remove the mirror and the image disappears. The image also disappears if you turn off all the light or if you close your eyes. Light must bounce off your body, bounce off the mirror, and enter your eyes. The bouncing of light from surfaces is called reflection. In this chapter, you will investigate the reflection of both light and sound.

Reflection of Light

Materials

- ✓ **an adult**
- ✓ mirror
- ✓ large, rigid shoe box
- ✓ light socket
- ✓ clear, 60-watt bulb that has a straight-line filament
- ✓ pencil
- ✓ sharp knife
- ✓ ruler
- ✓ black construction paper
- ✓ scissors
- ✓ tape
- ✓ sheet of white paper
- ✓ clay
- ✓ protractor
- ✓ white index card

When light "bounces" off a mirror, its path changes. We say the light has been reflected. To see exactly how light reflects, you can look at what happens to a ray (a narrow beam) of light when it strikes a mirror. To make a narrow beam of light, you can build a light box from a large, rigid shoe box, a light socket, and a clear, 60-watt bulb that has a straight-line filament (see Figure 13).

Place the socket at the middle of one end of the shoe box. Draw a line around the socket as shown in Figure 13a. **Ask an adult** to make a hole by cutting out the circle you have marked. Next, **ask the adult** to cut out a rectangle about 6 cm by 8 cm (2.5 in by 3 in) from the opposite end of the box (see Figure 13b). Put the socket through the round hole and attach the clear

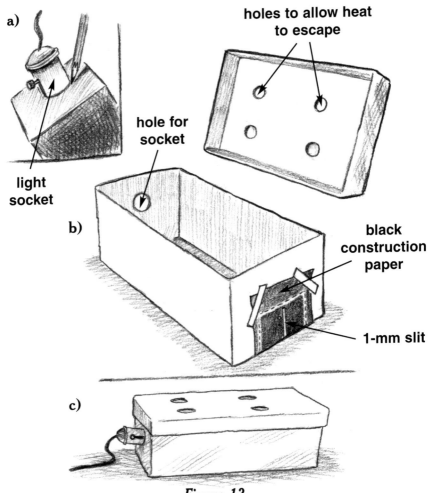

Figure 13.

a) Use a light socket to mark a circle on one end of a shoe box. Then have an adult cut out the circle.

b) Ask an adult to cut a rectangular opening in the opposite end of the box. Cover this opening with a piece of black paper in which you have made a very narrow slit. Ask an adult to cut holes in the top of the box to release heat from the bulb.

c) The completed light box.

lightbulb. Be sure the bulb's straight filament is vertical. Cut a piece of black construction paper a little larger than the rectangle. Cut a narrow (1-mm) vertical slit in it about 6 cm (2.5 in) long. Tape the piece of black paper over the rectangular opening. Finally, **ask the adult** to cut several holes in the shoe box's top. The holes will allow heat generated by the bulb to escape.

Put the top on the box. Place the box on a table or the floor and turn on the light. This is your completed light box (see Figure 13c).

When the light is on in the light box, you should see a narrow beam of light emerge through the narrow slit. Place a flat sheet of white paper in front of the narrow slit. The narrow beam of light can then be seen on the paper. Put a mirror upright on the white paper. You may need a piece of clay to keep the mirror upright. Place the base of a protractor against the mirror, as shown in Figure 14.

Arrange the mirror and protractor so that the narrow light beam strikes the mirror at the midpoint of the protractor's straight edge. A line perpendicular (at a right angle) to the mirror (the 90° line on the protractor) is called the normal. The angle between the beam going to the mirror and the normal is called the angle of incidence ($\angle i$). The angle between the normal and the reflected beam is called the angle of reflection ($\angle r$).

Move the mirror and protractor so as to produce a number of different angles of incidence. For each one, record the angle

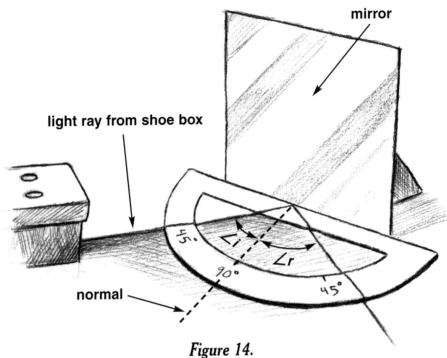

Figure 14.

In the drawing, angles *i* and *r* are both approximately 55 degrees. Remember, these angles are measured from the normal, a line perpendicular to the mirror at the point where the light ray strikes the mirror.

of incidence and the angle of reflection. How does each angle of incidence compare with its corresponding angle of reflection?

Replace the smooth, shiny surface of the mirror with a white index card. The card, although it feels smooth, has a much rougher surface than the mirror. What is different when you use the index card in place of the mirror? How does the light reflected from the card compare with the light reflected from the mirror?

Experiment 3.2

Mirrors, Reflection, and Images

Materials

- ✓ ruler
- ✓ small mirror
- ✓ table
- ✓ clay
- ✓ 2 pencils
- ✓ sheet of white paper
- ✓ a partner

As mentioned before, when you look into a mirror, you see your image. Light reflected by your body is reflected again by the mirror to produce the image you see. But where is the image you see in the mirror? Is it on the mirror? Or behind the mirror, as it appears to be? If you hold a ruler perpendicular to the mirror, the ruler's image appears to extend into the mirror as far as the actual ruler extends out from the mirror.

You can find out where the image really is. The technique involves looking at an object from two different angles. Hold one finger at an arm's length in front of your face. Hold the other finger close to your face. Now look at both fingers, first with your right eye and then with your left eye. You will see the position of the nearer finger shift relative to the distant finger. This shifting of one object relative to another when viewed from different positions is called parallax.

Now hold one finger on top of the other at an arm's length in front of your face. Again, close first one eye and then the other. This time the two fingers stay together; they do not shift relative to one another. We say there is no parallax between them. There is, however, parallax between the two fingers and more distant objects.

You can use lack of parallax to locate the image you see in a mirror. Stand a small mirror upright on a table. You may need a piece of clay to keep the mirror from tipping over. Use another piece of clay to support a pencil about 10 cm (4 in) in front of the mirror, as shown in Figure 15. Support a second pencil in the same way behind the mirror. Align your head behind the pencil in front of the mirror. You can now see the entire pencil in front of the mirror, its image in the mirror, and the top of the pencil behind the mirror. Have a partner move the pencil located behind the mirror until there is no parallax between it and the image of the pencil located in front of the mirror. When there is no parallax, you know the pencil behind the mirror is at the same place as the image of the pencil seen in the mirror.

Now measure the distances from the mirror to the pencil in front of the mirror, and to the pencil behind the mirror. How do these distances compare?

Repeat the experiment a number of times. Each time, place the pencil a different distance from the mirror. Then locate its image using the pencil behind the mirror. What can you conclude about the location of your own image when you look into a plane (flat) mirror?

Figure 15.

You can locate a mirror image by using parallax.

Hold a piece of white paper in front of your face. You do not see your image because the surface of the white paper is rough; consequently, it reflects light diffusely (in all directions). Because a mirror's surface is very smooth, it reflects any narrow light beam in only one direction, not many. It is the uniform reflection of light from a mirror that enables it to form clear images. You will see how this is done in the next experiment.

Science Project Idea

● Early Greek scholars believed that we see because light rays come out from our eyes, strike objects, and bounce back to our eyes. Design an experiment to show that light does not come out of people's eyes.

Experiment 3.3

A Model to Explain Mirror Images

Materials

- ✓ light box from Experiment 3.1
- ✓ scissors
- ✓ tape
- ✓ sheet of white paper
- ✓ a partner
- ✓ 2 mirrors
- ✓ ruler
- ✓ pencil

From the previous experiment, you know that light is reflected in an irregular or haphazard way by rough surfaces and in a very uniform way by smooth surfaces such as mirrors. Using the light box you made in Experiment 3.1, you can make a simple model to show how mirrors form clear images. With scissors, simply cut a second narrow slit about 1 cm to one side of the narrow slit already in the construction paper cover.

Retape this two-slit cover to the light box as shown in Figure 16a. Let the two narrow beams (rays) of light fall on a sheet of white paper.

Have a partner use a mirror to reflect one of the rays so that the two rays cross as shown. Let the point where the two rays cross represent a point *0* on an object from which two light rays have been reflected. Reflect these two rays using a second mirror as shown in Figure 16b. Notice that the two rays diverge (spread out) both before and after being reflected.

Use a ruler and pencil to draw lines on the white paper along the narrow beams (rays) of incident and reflected light going to and reflected from the second mirror. Then draw a line along the front of the second mirror. Remove the mirror and use your ruler and pencil to make dotted lines extending the two reflected rays. The point where they meet is where they would have appeared to meet behind the mirror (Figure 16c). Finally, measure the distance from the location of the mirror to the point behind the mirror where the rays appeared to meet. That point represents the position of the image. How do the distances from object (point *0*) to mirror and mirror to image compare?

The model you just made shows how two light rays from one point on an object are reflected to form just one point on an image, and that point appears to be behind the mirror. It appears to be where it is because your eye makes a guess. Your eye assumes the diverging rays originate where they appear to join at a point behind the mirror. With real objects, every point

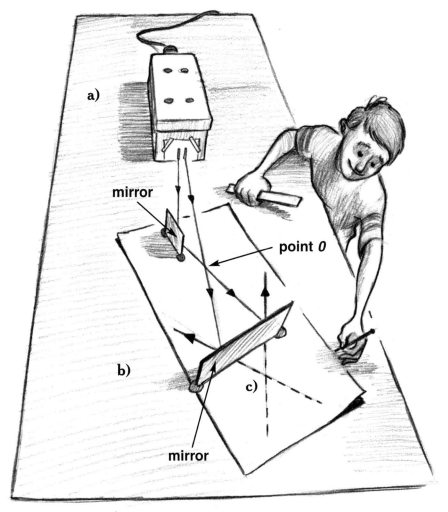

Figure 16.

a) A light box with two slits can form two rays of light. Reflect one ray with a mirror to form a point (*0*) where the two rays cross.

b) With a second mirror, reflect the rays coming from the point.

c) Use a ruler to extend the two reflected light rays to a point where they would meet behind the mirror.

on the object sends out countless rays. But the principle is the same for many points, each with many rays, as it is for one point with two rays. All the rays that strike the mirror from all the many points on the object are reflected to form an image. Rays of light from all the points on the object are reflected and appear to be coming from points behind the mirror. The combination of all these reflected rays produces a clear likeness of the object— a mirror image.

Science Project Ideas

- What problems confront you when you try to print a message that can be read as a mirror image?

- Place two mirrors upright and at right angles to one another. If you look into the mirrors, you will see three images of your face. Account for each image. What is different about the middle image? Why do you think it is different?

Experiment 3.4

Reflections From a Concave Mirror

Materials

- ✓ **an adult**
- ✓ concave mirror, such as a makeup or shaving mirror
- ✓ a sunny day
- ✓ room with a view of the outside
- ✓ a partner
- ✓ sheet of white cardboard
- ✓ meterstick or yardstick
- ✓ dark room
- ✓ candle
- ✓ matches

Ordinary plane mirrors are perfectly flat. Concave mirrors, on the other hand, bow inward like a very shallow dish (see Figure 17a). We know that when light is reflected, the angle of incidence equals the angle of reflection. Consequently, as Figure 17b shows, we would expect a concave mirror to bring light rays together. In fact, a concave mirror should bring the nearly parallel rays from a distant object together to form a clear image. The distance from the mirror to the points where the light rays come together to form an image is called the focal length of the mirror.

To see if this really happens, hold a concave mirror, such as a makeup or shaving mirror, several meters from a window. Turn the mirror toward a distant object seen through the window. Have a partner hold a sheet of white cardboard in

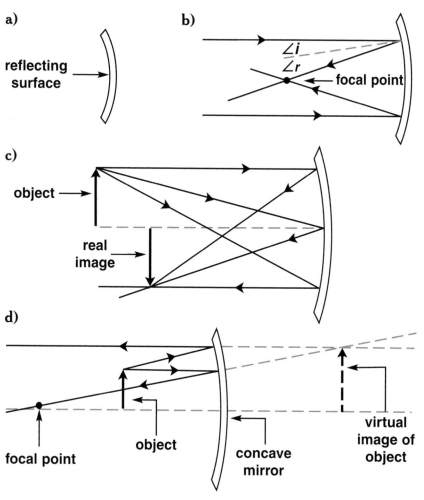

Figure 17.

a) A side view of a concave mirror.

b) A concave mirror should converge light, bringing parallel rays together at a point in front of the mirror.

c) We might expect a concave mirror to form real images.

d) The image of an object less than one focal length from a concave mirror will be virtual and appear larger than the object.

front of the mirror. Move the mirror toward and away from the cardboard. You will find a distance at which you see an image of the distant object on the cardboard. Is the image right-side up or inverted? The distance between the mirror and the cardboard is the focal length of the mirror. What is the approximate focal length of your mirror?

Unlike the virtual images you see in a plane (flat) mirror, the image formed on the cardboard screen by the concave mirror is really there. For that reason, such an image is called a *real image*.

Figure 17c would suggest that a concave mirror can form real images of nearby objects. To see if a concave mirror really can produce a real image of a nearby object, **ask an adult** to light a candle in a dark room. Hold the concave mirror slightly more than one focal length from the candle. Have a partner locate the real image of the candle flame by using a sheet of white cardboard to "capture" the image. What do you notice about the image?

Next, place the mirror about five focal lengths from the candle. How far is the image from the mirror now? How does the size of the image compare with the size of the flame? What happens to the size and location of the image as you move the mirror closer to the candle? What happens when you place the mirror less than one focal length from the candle? Can you find a real image?

In a bright room, what do you see when you place the mirror less than one focal length from your face? Can you see your image in the mirror? If you can, how does the size of your image compare with the size of your face?

The image you see when you hold a concave mirror less than one focal length from an object is a virtual image. It is similar to the images you see in a plane mirror. It appears to be where it is because your eye makes a guess. Your eye assumes the diverging rays originate where they appear to join at a point behind the mirror, as shown in Figure 17d.

Science Project Idea

● The surface of convex mirrors, such as the kind found on the right-hand side of automobiles, bulges outward like the bottom of a spoon. Obtain a convex mirror and examine the images it forms. Are the images real or virtual? Are they right-side up or inverted? How does the size of the images they form compare with the size of the objects from which they originate?

Experiment 3.5

Reflection of Sound

Materials

- ✓ table
- ✓ smooth wall
- ✓ 2 mailing tubes, 1–2 m long
- ✓ large sheet of paper
- ✓ protractor
- ✓ straight edge
- ✓ cassette or CD player with earphones
- ✓ towel
- ✓ mirror

In Experiment 3.1 you discovered how light is reflected. As you found, the angle of incidence always equals the angle of reflection. Does sound reflect in the same way?

To find out, find or place a table next to a smooth wall. Place two long mailing tubes on a large sheet of paper that rests on the table. Using a protractor and straight edge, draw two long lines on the paper, each 45 degrees from a line perpendicular to the wall. Arrange the two tubes so that they lie along the lines you have drawn. Place one earphone of a cassette or CD player into the end of one of the long tubes, as shown in Figure 18. Wrap the other earphone in a towel to absorb sound coming from it. Turn on the cassette or CD player and put your ear against the open end of the other tube. Can you hear music from the cassette or CD player? Is the sound as loud when you change the angle of either tube?

smooth wall

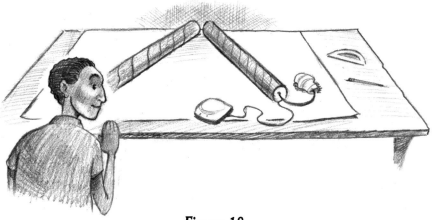

Figure 18.

Does sound reflect in the same way as light?

Place a mirror between the wall and the tubes. Does the mirror make the sound clearer than the wall?

Repeat the experiment with the tubes at equal angles other than 45 degrees. What do you find? What can you conclude about the reflection of sound? How is the reflection of sound similar to the reflection of light? How does the reflection of sound differ from the reflection of light?

Science Project Idea

● What is a sonic boom and what causes it?

Chapter 4

Light, Sound, and Refraction

When you look down into a swimming pool, it looks shallower than it actually is. Put a long pencil in a glass of water. From some angles the pencil will appear to be broken at the point where it enters the water. Look at the print on this page through a magnifying glass. The print will appear to be much larger than it actually is. These effects are caused by refraction—the bending of light when it passes at an angle from one medium, such as air, to another, such as water or glass. In this chapter, you will investigate the refraction of both light and sound.

Experiment 4.1

Refraction of Light

Materials

- ✓ light box from Experiment 3.1
- ✓ clear, plastic rectangular container
- ✓ sheet of white paper
- ✓ water
- ✓ pencil
- ✓ protractor
- ✓ ruler
- ✓ coin
- ✓ teacup
- ✓ a partner
- ✓ water glass

To see exactly how light refracts (bends), you can look at a ray of light as it enters water from air. You can use the light box you used in Experiment 3.1 to make a narrow beam of light.

Place a clear, plastic rectangular container on a sheet of white paper. Nearly fill the container with water. Draw lines along the long sides of the container. You will use these lines to measure the angles that light enters and leaves the water. Place the base of a protractor against the container as shown in Figure 19. Arrange the container and protractor so that the narrow beam of light from the light box strikes the water at the midpoint of the protractor's straight edge. The angle between the light beam going to the water and the normal, which is a line perpendicular (at a right angle) to the water (the 90° line on the protractor), is the angle of incidence ($\angle i$). To find the angle of refraction, mark the point where the light beam emerges from the other side of the water (see Figure 19). Carefully remove the container of water. Use a ruler to draw a line connecting the midpoint of the protractor and the point where the light beam emerged on the other side of the container. That line marks the path the light followed in the water.

To find the angle of refraction, measure the angle between the light path in the water and the normal setup at the point

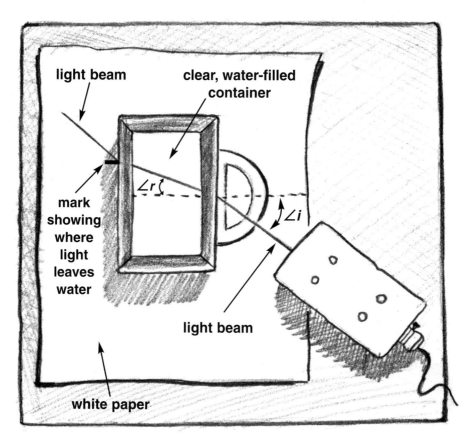

Figure 19.
An overhead view of Experiment 4.1

where the light entered the water. What is the angle of refraction? How does it compare with the angle of incidence? What is the ratio of the angle of incidence to the angle of refraction?

Repeat the experiment several times. Each time change the angle of incidence. What happens to the angle of refraction? What is the ratio of the angle of incidence to the angle of refraction in each case? At what angle of incidence is the light not refracted?

OTHER EXAMPLES OF LIGHT REFRACTION

✓ Place a coin in a teacup. Stand about a meter (yard) from the cup. Lower your head until the coin just disappears, hidden by the side of the cup. Ask a partner to slowly pour water into the cup, being careful not to disturb the coin. At a certain point, you will be able to see the coin again. Can you explain why the coin reappears when water is added?

✓ Put a coin on the bottom of a water glass. Look at the coin through the glass at an angle of about 45 degrees. Have a partner slowly pour water into the glass. You will see two coins, one of which seems to be rising toward the top of the glass. Can you explain what you observe?

✓ Put your finger into the center of a glass of water. Why do you think the submerged portion of your finger appears larger than the rest of it?

Science Project Idea

● Design and carry out an experiment to measure the angles of incidence and refraction when light passes from air to glass. Does glass bend light more, less, or the same as water? Does clear plastic bend light more, less, or the same as water?

Experiment 4.2

Refraction of Light by Lenses

Materials

- ✓ **an adult**
- ✓ room with a window
- ✓ convex lens with a focal length of 15–30 cm (a magnifying glass)
- ✓ clay
- ✓ meterstick or yardstick
- ✓ index card
- ✓ matches
- ✓ candle
- ✓ table
- ✓ a partner
- ✓ sheet of white cardboard
- ✓ concave lens

Lenses made of glass or plastic bend light. If you feel the surface of a lens, you will discover that it is curved. Convex lenses bulge outward. They are thickest in the middle. Concave lenses are thinner in the middle and thicker at their perimeters (see Figure 20a).

CONVEX LENSES

As you can see from Figure 20b, a convex lens converges light (brings it together). This convergence of light suggests that a convex lens can bring together light from an object to form an upside-down (inverted) image of the object. To see if this really happens, find a light-colored wall that is opposite a window with a view of the outside. Hold a convex lens near the wall. Can you form images of the outside view on the wall? Are the images of the objects seen in your view of the outside inverted?

The images you see are real images. Unlike the virtual images you see in a plane mirror, these images are really there. They can be seen on a screen.

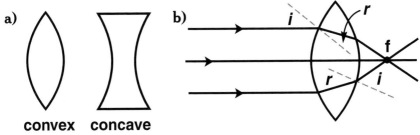

convex   concave

Figure 20.

a) Side views of convex and concave lenses.

b) A convex lens converges light. In the drawing, the light rays coming to the lens are parallel. They are brought together at a point called the focal point, f. The dotted lines are perpendicular to the surface of the lens so that angles *i* and *r* can be shown.

c)

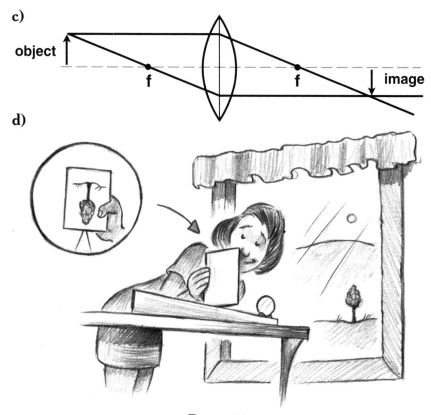

Figure 20.

c) Because a convex lens converges light, we can expect such a lens to produce inverted real images.

d) What is the focal length of your convex lens?

The focal length of a convex lens is the distance from the lens to the focal point. The focal point is where parallel rays of light are brought together. To obtain parallel rays of light, you can use a distant object such as a tree, a tall building, or any object that is far away. The rays from a distant object must be very nearly parallel because any diverging rays would not strike the lens.

To find the focal length of your convex lens, use a piece of clay to fix the lens to a meterstick or yardstick (see Figure 20d). Move an index card back and forth behind the lens until you obtain a clear image of a distant object. What is the distance between the lens and the image? What is the focal length of your convex lens?

To see that the focal length on both sides of a convex lens is the same, simply turn the lens around. Has the focal length changed?

In a dark room, **with an adult present**, light a candle on a table. Place a convex lens more than one focal length from the candle. Have a partner use a sheet of white cardboard to locate the image of the candle flame. What do you notice about the image? Place the lens exactly two focal lengths from the candle. What is the distance between the lens and the image? What happens to the size and location of the image as you move the lens closer to the candle? As you move the lens farther from the candle? What happens when you place the lens less than one focal length from the candle? Can you see an image if you look toward the candle through the lens?

The image you see when you hold the convex lens less than one focal length from the candle is a virtual image. It is similar to the images you see in a plane mirror. It appears to be where it is because your eye assumes the diverging rays originate where they appear to join at a point on the other side of the lens, as shown in Figure 21a.

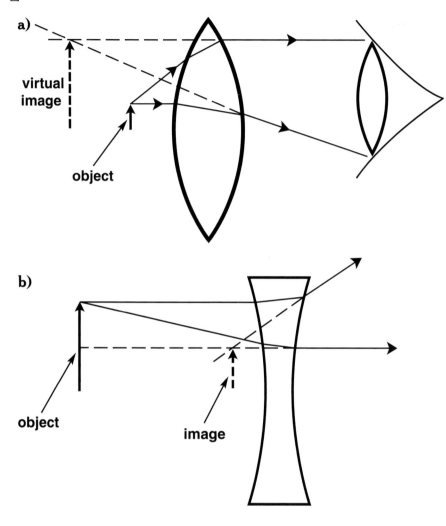

Figure 21.

a) A convex lens held close to an object produces an upright, magnified, virtual image of the object.

b) A convex lens diverges (spreads) light rays. Therefore, it can never form real images. Like mirror images, we see the images of concave lenses at the positions from which the diverging rays seem to be coming.

Hold the convex lens a few centimeters above the print on this page. How does the size of the virtual images you see compare with the size of the print? Can you explain why?

CONCAVE LENSES

Look at objects through a concave lens. Any images you see are virtual images because a concave lens diverges (spreads) light. Therefore, light rays passing through such a lens will never come together. See Figure 21b.

Examine an object carefully through a concave lens. Place the object at different distances from the lens. Is the image of an object seen through a concave lens ever as large or larger than the object? If not, can you explain why?

Science Project Ideas

- Design a method for locating the position of the virtual images seen through a concave lens.

- Examine a camera used to take photographs. One of its major components is a convex lens. How does the camera work? What is the purpose of the shutter? How is a camera similar to the human eye? How is it different from the eye?

Experiment 4.3

Refraction of Sound

Materials

✓ large balloon

✓ vinegar

✓ seltzer tablets

✓ plastic flask

✓ electronic buzzer, 3,000–
4,000 Hz (available at
electronics stores)

✓ table

✓ tape measure

✓ a partner

✓ towels

✓ twistie

The refraction of sound is more difficult to detect than the refraction of light. We cannot see sound bend. However, we do know that sound travels faster through warm air than through cold air. At night, near a large body of water, you can often hear distant sounds that are not detectable during the day. The reason for this is that at night, air close to the water is colder than air higher up. As a result, sound waves reaching the warmer upper air are bent down, as shown in Figure 22a. During the day, air close to the water is often warmer than air higher up, causing sound waves to bend upward (see Figure 22b).

Sound also travels faster in air than in carbon dioxide. Sound will bend when it travels from air to carbon dioxide. In

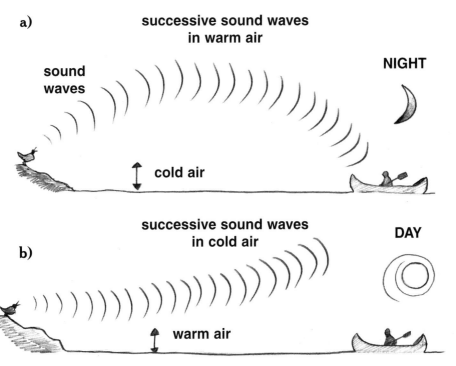

Figure 22.

Sound travels faster in warm air than in cold air. As a result, sound waves are bent (refracted) where warm air and cold air meet.

fact, you can make a carbon dioxide lens that will bend sound coming through air.

A balloon filled with carbon dioxide can serve as a convex lens. To inflate the balloon, add vinegar to several seltzer tablets in a plastic flask. Then pull the neck of the balloon over the mouth of the flask (see Figure 23a). When the balloon stops inflating, seal the balloon's neck with a twistie.

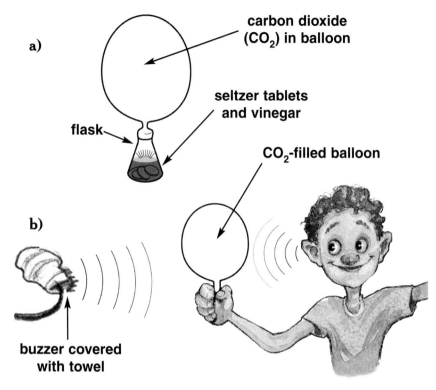

Figure 23.

a) A balloon is filled with carbon dioxide gas.

b) The balloon serves as a lens that will converge sound waves.

Place an electronic buzzer on a table about 4 to 5 meters (13 to 16 ft) from where you will stand. Have a partner cover the buzzer with towels until you can barely hear it. Then have your partner move the carbon dioxide lens (balloon) slowly toward your ear (see Figure 23b). When the sound is loudest, your ear is at the point where some of the sound waves are converging. How far is the balloon from your ear when this happens?

Chapter 5

Dispersion, Light, and Color

As you saw in Chapter 4, light is refracted when it passes at an angle from one transparent material to another. For example, light is bent as it passes from air to water or glass. In this chapter, you will look more closely at refracted light. You will find, as did Sir Isaac Newton, that ordinary white light can be separated into different colors by refraction.

Experiment 5.1

Prisms, Refraction, and Dispersion

Materials

- ✓ glass or plastic prism
- ✓ sunlight
- ✓ light-colored wall
- ✓ water
- ✓ clear, plastic rectangular container

- ✓ light box from Experiment 3.1
- ✓ dark room
- ✓ sheet of white paper
- ✓ tape
- ✓ clear plastic jar

Hold and turn a glass or plastic prism in sunlight. Let the refracted light fall on a light-colored wall. You will soon find a spectrum, a rainbow of colors, on the wall. Repeat the experiment with a closed, clear, rectangular container that is filled with water. You should be able to obtain a similar spectrum by turning the water-filled container.

To see how a spectrum of colors is obtained from ordinary white light, you will need the light box you made in Experiment 3.1 with the one-ray slit, a prism, and a clear, rectangular water-filled container. In a dark room, place the prism on a sheet of white paper in front of the light box, as shown in Figure 24a. Let the light ray strike the prism near its tip at a large angle of incidence. Look at the beam of light that emerges. What has happened to the white light? Are all colors of light

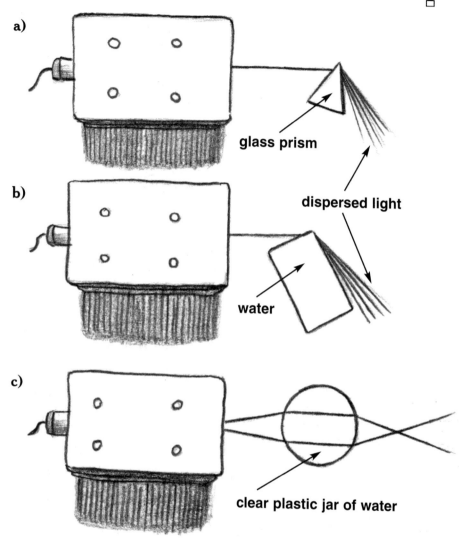

a)

glass prism

dispersed light

b)

water

c)

clear plastic jar of water

Figure 24.

a) A glass or plastic prism can be used to separate white light by refraction into the colors of which it is composed.

b) Water can also refract light into a spectrum.

c) A similar, but less obvious, effect is seen when a lens refracts light.

refracted by the same amount? If not, which color is refracted the most? Which color is refracted the least?

Repeat the experiment using a clear rectangular container of water (see Figure 24b). Can you obtain a spectrum using a water "prism"? Which color is refracted the most by water? Which color is refracted the least?

Tape a two-slit cover over the opening in the light box so that two rays of light emerge. Fill a clear plastic jar with water to serve as a two-dimensional model of a lens. Use the lens to form an "image" as shown in Figure 24c. Which color is refracted most by the lens? Which color is refracted least?

The difference in the amount that light of different colors is refracted is called dispersion. We say white light is dispersed into its component colors when refracted by glass, water, or other transparent materials. It is dispersion that gives rise to rainbows. Dispersion is also a problem for inexpensive lenses, which often form images with a ring of mixed colors along their edges.

Science Project Ideas

- What are coronas, halos, and "mock suns" or "sun dogs"? How are they related to dispersion or refraction?

- On a sunny day, use a water hose with a spray nozzle to see if you can make a miniature rainbow.

Experiment 5.2

Mixing Colored Lights

Materials

✓ **an adult**

✓ dark room

✓ 3 light sockets

✓ white wall

✓ one or more electrical outlets

✓ 25-watt red, green, and blue bulbs (available at supermarkets)

Can the colors separated by dispersion be put back together to make white light? To find out, you will need a very dark room. To begin, place three light sockets near a white wall. **Ask an adult** to connect them to one or more electrical outlets. (You may need an extension cord with multiple outlets if only one wall outlet is available.) Screw 25-watt red, green, and blue bulbs into the three sockets (see Figure 25). What is the color of the wall when illuminated by only the red bulb? When illuminated by only the blue bulb? By only the green bulb?

When all three bulbs are lit, you should find that the central area of the wall that is illuminated by all three bulbs is white. Since the light intensity from all three bulbs may not be equal, you may have to move one or more bulbs closer or farther from the wall to produce white light.

Now, light the wall with both the green and the blue bulbs. The color you see on the wall is called cyan. You might call it blue-green. When you illuminate the wall with the red and blue

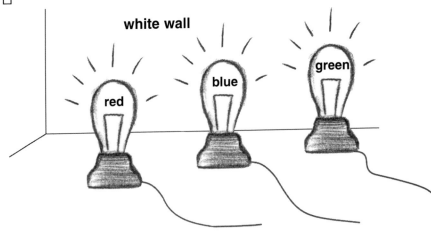

Figure 25.

To mix colored lights, place three colored lightbulbs (red, green, and blue) near a white wall.

bulbs, the color you see is called magenta. You might call it purple. What color do you see when the green and red bulbs light the wall? If you have difficulty determining the color, turn off one light and then turn it back on.

Science Project Idea

- You can mix colored lights by modifying the light box you built in Experiment 3.1. Make a cover that has 2-cm-wide openings covered with transparent red, blue, and green filters. Then mix the colors on white paper using mirrors to reflect the colored beams. You can obtain color filters from Edmund Scientifics Company (see Appendix).

Experiment 5.3

Colored Shadows

Materials

- ✓ colored bulbs, light sockets, and electrical outlets used in Experiment 5.2
- ✓ yardstick
- ✓ white wall
- ✓ dark room
- ✓ cardboard
- ✓ scissors

You can use the colored bulbs you used in Experiment 5.2 to cast shadows of objects. With just the red bulb turned on, hold a yardstick between the bulb and the wall. The stick's shadow is black, as you can see. What do you predict the color of the shadow will be if only the blue light is turned on? If only the green light is turned on?

Next, turn on the red bulb and the green bulb. How many shadows does the stick cast now? What is the color of each one? Which light casts which shadow? Which light illuminates which shadow?

Repeat the experiment with the red bulb and the blue bulb turned on. Which light casts which shadow? Which light illuminates which shadow?

If you turn on only the green and blue bulbs, which light casts which shadow? Which light illuminates which shadow?

Predict the number of shadows cast by the stick and the color of each one when all three bulbs are turned on. Then try it. Was your prediction about the number of shadows correct? What about the colors?

If you did not predict the colors correctly, can you now explain why each shadow has the color it does?

Just for fun, hold your hands between the three bulbs and the wall. How many colored shadows do you see? Why are some parts of the shadows black?

A SHADOW THAT TURNS

Using scissors, cut an arrow about 15 cm (6 in) by 5 cm (2 in) from cardboard. Turn on the red and green lightbulbs. Hold the arrow between the bulbs and the white wall. Do the shadows have the colors you expected? In which direction do the shadows of the arrow point?

Now hold the arrow so that it points away from the wall and toward the bulbs. In which direction do the shadows of the arrow point now? How can you hold the arrow so that its shadows point toward one another?

Sound, Light, and Waves

You have seen that both sound and light can be reflected and refracted. In Chapter 1, you learned that longitudinal waves can be used to explain the behavior of sound. If waves can explain the behavior of sound, perhaps they can also explain the behavior of light. But before we draw such a conclusion, we need to see if waves, such as water waves, reflect and refract. To do that you can use a ripple tank. If your school has one, you might ask to borrow it. Or you can make a simple tank of your own as described in Experiment 6.1.

Experiment 6.1

Reflected Waves

Materials

- ✓ **an adult**
- ✓ ripple tank or a large glass baking dish, or a plastic sweater box, or any similar large, shallow, transparent container
- ✓ chairs or boxes
- ✓ white paper or cardboard
- ✓ water
- ✓ ruler
- ✓ lightbulb, preferably a point source of light like the one used in Experiment 2.3
- ✓ table or bookshelf
- ✓ yardstick
- ✓ duct tape
- ✓ strips of cloth such as gauze or foam tubing
- ✓ wood or paraffin block
- ✓ wood dowel, about 1 inch diameter
- ✓ piece of thick rubber hose
- ✓ piece of thick wire (optional)

Do this experiment under **adult supervision**. If you do not have access to a ripple tank, you can make one of your own. A large glass baking dish, a plastic sweater box, or any similar large, shallow, transparent container can be used. Chairs or boxes can support the ripple tank about half a meter above a screen of white paper or cardboard, as shown in Figure 26. Be sure the tank is level. Add water to a depth of about one centimeter (half an inch). If the tank is level, the water will be the same depth everywhere in the tank.

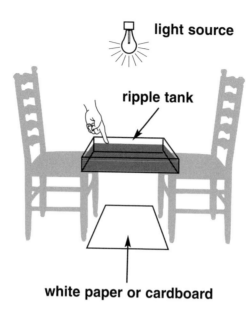

light source

ripple tank

white paper or cardboard

Figure 26.

A ripple tank can be made from simple materials.

The water should be illuminated from above by a lightbulb, preferably a point source of light like the one you used in Experiment 2.3. Be sure the light source is secured to a table or bookshelf. You can use a yardstick and duct tape to extend the bulb over the water. **Never let the bulb or socket touch the water. Never touch the bulb or socket and the water at the same time.**

Dip your finger into the water. You will see an image of the water wave you generate on the white paper screen below the tank. What is the shape of the wave? What happens to the wave when it reaches the edges of the tank?

You can reduce wave reflections from the sides of the tank by lining the outer walls of the tank with strips of cloth such as gauze or foam tubing.

Place a wood or paraffin block in the tank to represent a mirror. Use a wood dowel resting on the bottom of the tank to make a wave (see Figure 27a). Simply roll the dowel a very short distance toward you with your fingertips. Watch the image of the wave on the screen. The wave can be thought of as a large number of closely packed rays traveling outward from the dowel. What happens when the wave reaches the "mirror"? Is it reflected?

Change the angle at which the wave hits the "mirror," as shown in Figure 27b. Does this change the angle at which the wave is reflected? Does the angle of incidence appear to be equal to the angle of reflection?

Now, as shown in Figure 27c, dip your finger into the water in front of the "mirror." Think of the circular wave you produce as coming from a point of light, like the point of light in Figure 16 (Experiment 3.3). Look at the wave reflected from the "mirror." Where does it appear to be coming from? How is it like the mirror image you investigated in Experiments 3.2 and 3.3? Does the position of the "image" change if you move the "point of light" closer to the "mirror"? If you move it farther from the "mirror"?

You know that a concave mirror can converge light. To see how waves are reflected by a concave surface, place a piece of thick rubber hose in your ripple tank (see Figure 27d). If the hose is not curved, insert a heavy piece of wire into the hose and bend it. Use the dowel to send a straight wave toward the concave "mirror," as shown. Watch the wave converge at a focal point in front of the "mirror."

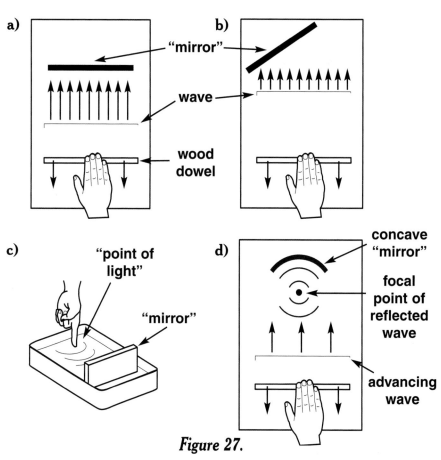

Figure 27.

A ripple tank seen from above when a) an experimenter makes a wave front; b) a wave front approaches a "mirror" at an angle; c) waves from a point source of waves approach a "mirror"; d) a concave "mirror" converges waves to a focal point.

Using your finger, make a point source of waves about two focal lengths in front of the "mirror." Can you find a real "image" of the point source at about the same place? What happens to the location of the "image" as you move the point source closer to the "mirror"? As you move it farther from the "mirror"?

Science Project Idea

● Place the point source of a wave one focal length from the concave "mirror" you used in the ripple tank in Experiment 6.1. What do you notice about the reflected waves? Use what you have observed to make a spotlight, that is, a light that produces a parallel beam of light.

Experiment 6.2

Refracted Waves

Materials

- ✓ ripple tank from Experiment 6.1
- ✓ ruler
- ✓ wood dowel
- ✓ flat, transparent glass or plastic plates, or plastic sandwich box
- ✓ thin wood blocks

Light and sound refract when passing from one medium to another. Do water waves refract?

Because liquids mix or layer when put together, we cannot easily transfer waves from one medium to another. However, we can see what happens when waves move from deep water into shallow water.

Make a section of your ripple tank shallow by stacking flat, transparent glass or plastic plates, as shown in Figure 28a. Or place a water-filled plastic sandwich box at one end of the tank. The shallow layer of water should only be about 1 to 3 mm deep. You will probably have to add water to make it deep enough to cover the shallow area.

Arrange the shallow-water region so that it is at an angle to straight waves you make with the wood dowel. Place thin wood blocks on either side of the shallow water (see Figure 28b). The blocks will deflect distracting portions of the waves that pass from deep to shallow water. Do the waves bend when they pass from deep to shallow water? Can water waves be refracted?

Science Project Idea

- Make a convex, lens-shaped area of shallow water in your ripple tank. Can waves be made to converge to a focal point by such a "lens"?

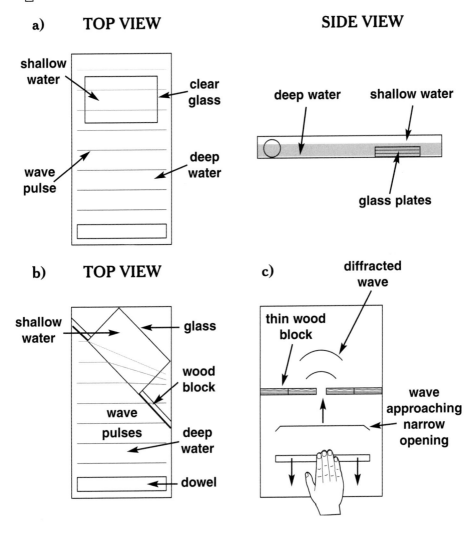

Figure 28.

a) Make a region of shallow water near one end of a ripple tank.

b) An overhead view of the ripple tank shows a wave in deep water as it approaches shallow water. Will the wave bend as it enters the shallow water?

c) Overhead view of diffraction in a ripple tank.

Experiment 6.3

Diffraction of Waves

Materials

✓ ripple tank from Experiment 6.1
✓ thin wood blocks
✓ wood dowel

Stand thin wood blocks across the center of your ripple tank, as shown in Figure 28c. Leave a narrow space between the two middle blocks. Then generate a wave with the wood dowel. Notice that, as the wave passes through the opening, it acts like a point source of new waves. These waves spread out on the other side of the block.

Does the same effect take place if you produce a series of equally spaced waves, one after the other?

What happens if you make the opening larger? If you make it smaller?

Next, stand the wood dowel on end in the center of the tank. Use your finger to make a point source of waves to one side of the dowel. Notice how the waves bend around the dowel.

The spreading out or bending of waves as they pass through a narrow opening or around an object is known as diffraction. Does sound diffract? Does light diffract? You can investigate those questions in the next experiment.

Experiment 6.4

Diffraction, Sound, and Light

Materials

- ✓ hallway adjacent to a room with a door
- ✓ a partner
- ✓ middle-C tuning fork
- ✓ long desk or table
- ✓ electronic buzzer like the one used in Experiment 4.3
- ✓ clear showcase bulb with straight, upright filament
- ✓ 2 opaque objects with straight edges, such as tongue depressors or small mirrors

As you saw in the previous experiment, water waves diffract around small objects. They also diffract when they pass through small openings.

SOUND AND DIFFRACTION

The diffraction of sound waves is easily observed. Simply stand in a hallway outside a room with an open door. Have someone inside the room talk to you. Then move down the hallway so that you are beyond the open door. Can you still hear the person? What leads you to believe that sound waves diffract?

You can carry out a more refined experiment by using sound waves of constant frequency. A middle-C tuning fork, which vibrates at 256 Hz, will produce sounds with a wavelength of about 1.3 m (about 4 ft).

Have a partner hold the vibrating tuning fork at one end of a desk or long table while you stand at the opposite end. With your ear turned toward the sound, lower your head until it is well below the edge of the table. If sound diffracts, you should notice very little change in sound intensity as you lower your head. If there is little or no diffraction, you will detect a definite loss of intensity as your head moves below the level of the table. What can you conclude about the diffraction of sound?

Next, repeat the experiment with an electronic buzzer like the one you used in Experiment 4.3. The buzzer should have a frequency of 3,000 Hz or higher, more than ten times greater than the tuning fork. At this higher frequency, do you detect a decrease in the loudness of the sound when you lower your ear below the table? Does diffraction appear to be related to the frequency of the sound?

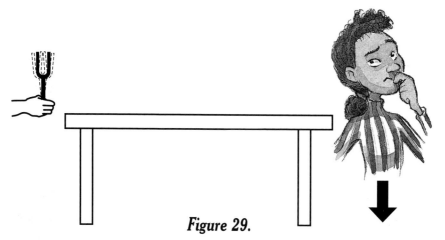

Figure 29.

You can use a table and a tuning fork to test whether or not sound diffracts.

LIGHT AND DIFFRACTION

Does light diffract? The fact that light casts sharp shadows might lead you to believe that light does not diffract. But before you decide that light is not wavelike, try the following experiment. Look at the bright line filament of an upright showcase bulb like the one shown in Figure 30. Close one eye and slowly bring together the first two fingers of one hand in front of your open eye. You will see the line of light spread out and eventually form a series of bright-colored bands.

To see the effect more clearly, bring two opaque objects with straight edges close together. You might use two tongue depressors or two small mirrors. As the width of the open slit between the edges becomes very small, you will see the light spread out. When the width of the slit is less than 0.1 mm, you will see bright bands of light with dark bands in between. The diffraction of light is evident when light passes through very narrow openings or around very small objects.

Science Project Ideas

- In the summer, people drive cars with their windows open. Many times the radio or CD player within the car can be heard from a distance. Why do you more often hear bass notes from these cars rather than sounds with higher frequencies?

Figure 30.

Examine the light from the long vertical filament of a showcase lightbulb. Let the light pass through a narrow slit between your fingers.

● Investigate the sounds made by whales. Whales make sounds that have both low and high frequencies, but the sounds have different purposes. It is believed that whales, like bats, use reflected sound waves just as we use sonar to locate objects around them in the deep, dark sea. Would whales be more likely to use high or low frequencies to detect objects? Why?

WAVES: A MODEL FOR SOUND AND LIGHT

As you have seen, both sound and light behave like waves in many ways: Waves reflect; so do sound and light. Waves refract; so do sound and light. Waves diffract; so do sound and light. It seems reasonable to use waves as a model for explaining the behavior of both light and sound. Perhaps, we can even use waves to predict behaviors about sound and light that you have not yet detected.

For example, suppose waves of a constant frequency were to pass through two or more narrow openings that were close together. Each opening would create a new point source of waves. What do you think would happen if waves from the two sources were to overlap? You will examine the overlapping of waves in the next two experiments.

Experiment 6.5

Overlap of Waves on a Slinky

Materials

✓ 2 partners

✓ a long Slinky

✓ a long, smooth floor

✓ several paper cups

Ask a partner to hold one end of a long Slinky while you generate a transverse pulse at the other end as you did in

Experiment 1.6. Then let your partner generate a pulse that resembles the one you made.

Now have your friend generate a pulse at the same time you do. Try to make both pulses as similar in size and shape as possible. The two pulses should meet at the middle of the Slinky. Do the waves pass through each other like beams of light do (for example, they cross in Experiment 3.3)?

What happens to the size of the pulses when they meet? This may be hard to observe because the pulses move fast. To overcome that difficulty, ask a third person to estimate how far your wave pulse moves sideways at the Slinky's midpoint. Have that person put several paper cups upside down on the floor far enough out to be beyond the sideways movement of your wave pulse. When you generate a pulse, the Slinky should not quite touch the cups. Similarly, a pulse generated by your partner should not quite touch the cups.

Now you and your friend should generate pulses as nearly identical as possible at the same time on the same side of the Slinky. This will produce two pulses like those shown in Figure 31a. What happens to the cups when the two pulses meet? Estimate the size of the combined pulses when they overlap.

Next, you and your partner should generate identical pulses at the same time on opposite sides of the Slinky. This will produce two pulses like those shown in Figure 31b. Try to predict what will happen when these pulses meet. Then arrange the cups to test your prediction and do the necessary experiment. Was your prediction correct?

Have your partner hold his end of the Slinky firmly in place. With one end of the Slinky fixed, the waves you generate will be reflected and overlap later waves you produce. You will find that you can make periodic waves (waves produced at regular intervals of time) that have nodes (points where there is no motion of the Slinky). Waves, such as these, made by overlapping waves of the same frequency traveling in opposite directions are called standing waves (see Figure 31c). Between the nodes are regions called maxima. There the wave amplitudes are large because the waves you make and the reflected waves come together. This doubles the size of crests and troughs.

In this experiment, you examined what happens when two wave pulses moving along a line combine. As you saw, these waves add to one another or cancel one another. Their action depends on whether they are on the same or opposite sides of the Slinky. The displacement of the Slinky when such pulses overlap is shown in Figure 32. As you can see, two wave crests will reinforce each other and double the amplitude of the wave; a wave crest combined with a corresponding wave trough will cancel one another, leaving the Slinky undisturbed with an amplitude of zero. The reinforcement or cancellation of one wave by another is called interference.

But what happens if periodic water waves pass through two or more narrow slits? Figure 33 shows waves diffracting at

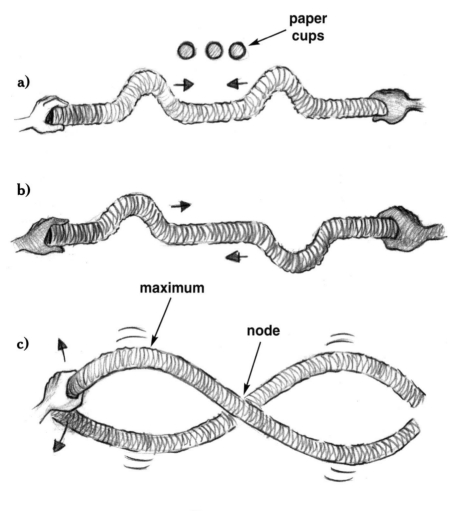

Figure 31.

a) What happens to the size of transverse pulses when they overlap?

b) What happens when opposite transverse pulses overlap?

c) You can make standing waves that have nodes where the amplitude is always zero. Between the nodes will be maxima where the amplitudes of crests and troughs are very large.

a)

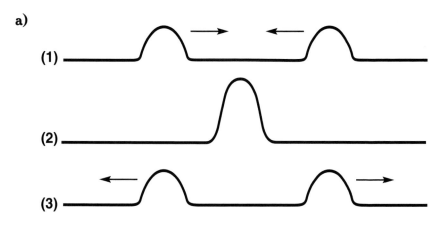

b)

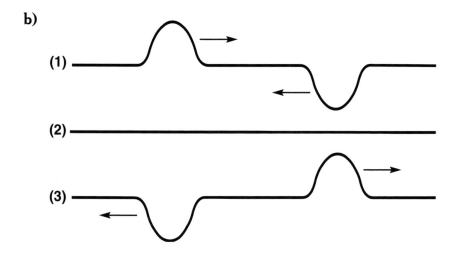

Figure 32.

Wave pulses on Slinkies in (a) and (b) are shown as they move from positions 1 through 3. a) When these two pulses overlap at position 2, the displacement of the Slinky doubles. b) When these two pulses overlap at position 2, the displacement of the Slinky is zero. After pulses cross, as seen in position 3 for both (a) and (b), they continue to move in the direction each was going before they met.

two slits (S_1 and S_2) that are close to one another. The crests are shown as dark lines. The troughs, which lie midway between crests, are unmarked. Where crests from one point source fall on crests from the other point source, wave amplitudes are large. Where crests from one source lie on troughs from the other source, amplitudes are zero. As you can see in Figure 33, the overlapping of crests and troughs from two sources of periodic waves creates an interference pattern. In this pattern, there are lines along which the displacement is always zero. These nodal lines of zero wave amplitude radiate from a point between the sources.

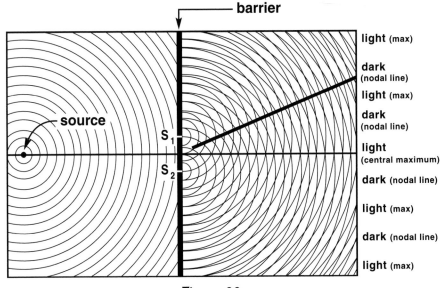

Figure 33.

This drawing shows how two overlapping sets of waves are formed when periodic waves pass through two narrow slits that are close together. If these waves were light waves, the nodal lines would be dark and the maxima would be bright light.

Experiment 6.6

Interference and Light

Materials

- ✓ showcase bulb
- ✓ fine-toothed comb
- ✓ diffraction grating
- ✓ a partner
- ✓ meterstick or yardstick
- ✓ compact disk (CD)

Can we find evidence of interference using light? To find out, look at the bright line filament of a showcase bulb through a comb. The narrow openings between the comb's teeth causes light to diffract, creating an interference pattern. You will see bands of bright light (maxima) separated by dark spaces (nodal lines). Turn the comb slightly to reduce the size of the open spaces through which the light passes. You will see the pattern spread out more.

Next, view the same showcase bulb through a diffraction grating. You may be able to borrow a diffraction grating from your school's science department. You can also purchase inexpensive diffraction gratings from a science supply company (see the Appendix). These gratings have about 5,300 lines per centimeter (13,400 lines per inch). With such narrow openings (about 0.00019 cm each), the interference pattern is very spread out. You will see what is called the central maximum at the bulb's filament. To either side, you will see a bright spectrum called the first maximum. The first maximum is separated from the central maximum by a wide, dark node. Which color in the spectrum is located closest to the central maximum? Which color in the spectrum is farthest from the central maximum?

If you look farther to each side, you will see a second spectrum, the second maximum. Which color in this maximum is closest to the central maximum? Which color is farthest from the central maximum?

The fact that you can see an interference pattern with light adds to the evidence that light behaves like waves. In fact, you can use the interference pattern you see with a diffraction grating to find the wavelength of light. If you go on to study physics, you will be able to deduce the following method for determining wavelength from the interference pattern seen through a diffraction grating.

The wavelength of a particular color in the first maximum is equal to the distance between the slits in the grating (d) times the distance of the color from the central maximum (x) divided by the distance of the grating from the color in the first maximum (L). (See Figure 34.)

Have a partner hold a meterstick or yardstick horizontally above the showcase bulb, while you stand about 0.5 meter (1.5 ft) in front of the bulb. As you look through the grating, have your partner move her finger along the stick until it lies over the color whose wavelength you want to measure. Have your partner record that distance from the bulb's filament. Then she can measure the distance from that color on the spectrum you see to the grating you are holding.

Use the formula Wavelength $= dx \div L$ to find the approximate wavelength of blue, green, and red light. Which of these wavelengths is the longest? Which is the shortest?

A compact disk (CD) or long-playing record (LP) has many grooves that are very close together. Use a CD or vinyl record to reflect artificial light **(not sunlight because it is dangerous)** to your eye. How can you tell that reflected light can also be used to produce interference patterns?

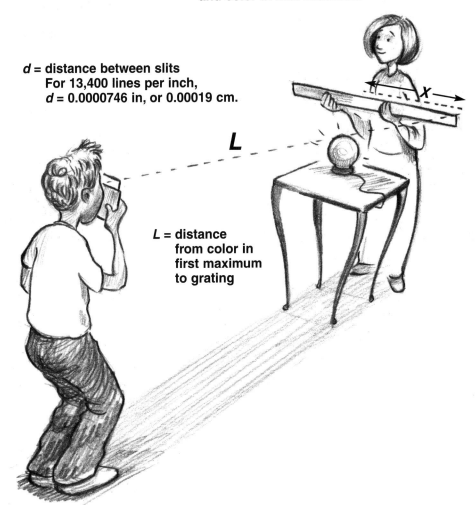

x = distance between central maximum and color in first maximum

d = distance between slits
For 13,400 lines per inch, d = 0.0000746 in, or 0.00019 cm.

L

X

L = distance from color in first maximum to grating

Figure 34.

When light passes through the narrow slits in a diffraction grating, an interference pattern is formed. To find the wavelength of a particular color in the first maximum of that pattern, you can use the formula Wavelength = dx/L.

Experiment 6.7

Interference and Sound

Materials

- ✓ audio oscillator (you may be able to borrow one from your school's science department)
- ✓ long extension cord
- ✓ building with a smooth, hard-surfaced wall
- ✓ meterstick or yardstick
- ✓ electronic buzzer used in Experiment 4.3
- ✓ 100-cm (40-in) and 50-cm (20-in) lengths of 5-cm- (2-in-) diameter PVC pipe (available at hardware store)
- ✓ newspapers
- ✓ rubber bands
- ✓ a partner

Since we used waves to explain the transmission of sound in Chapter 1, we can anticipate finding interference patterns with sound.

If possible, borrow an audio oscillator from your school's science department. With permission, place the oscillator outdoors. Working outdoors will prevent the distracting reflections of sound that occur indoors. You will need a long extension cord. Adjust the audio oscillator to about 1,000 Hz. Then turn the speaker toward a smooth, hard-surfaced wall several meters (yards) away. The reflection of the waves from the wall should produce standing waves. You made standing waves on a Slinky in Experiment 6.5.

The wavelength of a sound with a frequency of 1,000 Hz will be about 33 cm. Since nodes occur at intervals of half a wavelength, you can expect to find nodes at approximately 15- to 18-cm intervals. Can you find the nodes (minimal loudness) and maxima (maximum loudness) by moving your ear slowly back and forth between the speaker and the wall?

If the audio oscillator has two speakers, place them about 50 cm (20 in) apart in an open area. Set the frequency of the oscillator to about 2,500 Hz. Then slowly move your ear across the area in front of the speakers. We can expect sound waves of the same frequency coming from the two speakers to diffract and produce an interference pattern. Can you find nodes? Can you find maxima?

Predict what will happen to the number of nodal lines if you increase or decrease the frequency of the sound waves. Try it! Were your predictions correct?

What happens to the number of nodal lines when you separate the speakers by a greater distance? What do you predict will happen to the number of nodal lines if you bring the speakers closer together?

Place the electronic buzzer you used in Experiment 4.3 at the center of a 100-cm (40 in) length of PVC pipe that has a diameter of 5 cm (2 in). Wrap the tube with thick layers of newspaper held in place by rubber bands. The paper will absorb sound so that diffracting sound waves will come only from the ends of the tube.

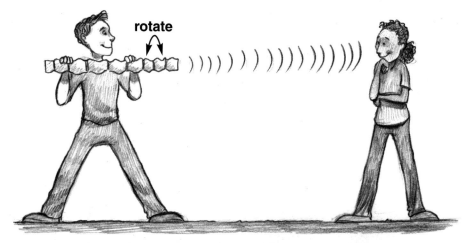

Figure 35.

Can you detect the interference of sound waves?

Stand outside several meters (yards) from the pipe. With the buzzer sounding, have a partner slowly rotate the pipe as shown in Figure 35. Can you detect sounds of maximum and minimum loudness as the pipe is rotated?

What happens to the number of maxima and nodal lines if you use a shorter pipe?

Science Project Idea

● Why must two sources of waves have the same frequency to produce an interference pattern?

Chapter 7

Transverse Waves and Polarized Light

The experiments you have done have probably convinced you that light consists of waves. But are these waves transverse (see p. 24), or are they longitudinal like sound waves? If light waves are transverse, they should oscillate in all planes. Transverse waves that do not oscillate in all planes are called polarized waves. Figure 36a shows an end-on view of a wave. If the wave oscillates in more than one of any of the 360 degrees possible, we would say the wave is not polarized. If, however, the wave oscillates in only one direction, as shown in Figures 36b and 36c, then the wave is polarized. If light waves can be

a)

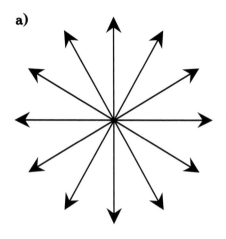

Figure 36.

a) An end view of a transverse wave that can oscillate in any plane perpendicular to its direction of motion.

b) A polarized transverse wave that oscillates only in the vertical plane.

c) A polarized transverse wave that oscillates only in the horizontal plane.

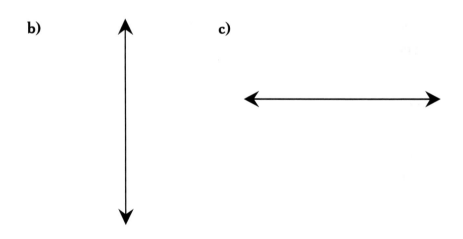

b)

c)

made to exhibit polarization, we can conclude that they are transverse. Longitudinal waves, by their very nature, cannot be polarized.

Polarizing Transverse Waves on a Rope

Materials

- ✓ long piece of rope, such as clothesline
- ✓ a partner
- ✓ board with a slot (see Figure 37)

You can use a long piece of rope such as clothesline to make transverse waves. Have a partner hold one end of the rope while you generate transverse waves from the other end. You can send a transverse wave along a rope by moving your hand up and down, right to left, or at any angle you choose. In fact, you can choose all possible angles for the wave by moving your hand in a small circle as if you were turning a jump rope. If, however, you send a wave along a rope by moving your hand up and down, the wave is polarized because it is moving in only one of the many possible planes available to it.

Here is a way to polarize a transverse wave on a rope. Turn the rope so that the wave moves along all possible transverse axes; that is, turn the rope as you might a jump rope. Make the wave pass through a slot in a board, as shown in Figure 37. If the slot is oriented vertically, only the vertical part of the rope's wave motion will be transmitted. If the slot is horizontal, only

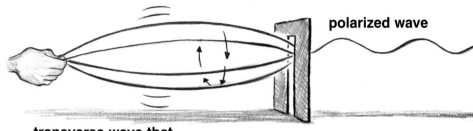

polarized wave

transverse wave that
is not polarized

Figure 37.

A slot in a board can change a nonpolarized wave on a rope
into one that is polarized.

horizontal waves will be transmitted. Waves vibrating in all
other directions will be removed by the slotted board.

Experiment 7.2

Polarizing Sheets or Glasses

Materials

✓ 2 pairs of polarizing sunglasses
or 2 sheets of polarizing film

In 1932, Edwin Land, an American industrialist, invented
polarizing sheets, now sold under the trademark Polaroid, by
embedding tiny needlelike crystals of quinine iodosulfate in thin
plastic film. To see what these polarizing sheets do to light, you
will need two pairs of polarizing sunglasses or two sheets of
polarizing film. If you use sunglasses, be sure they are marked
Polaroid. Some sunglasses simply reduce light intensity.

Polarizing film can be purchased from a science supply company, or you may be able to borrow some from your school's science department.

Look at the light coming through a window with one lens of a pair of sunglasses or one of the sheets of polarizing film (see Figure 38). You will see that the intensity of the light is reduced. Now place a second lens or film in front of the first one. Slowly rotate the second lens or film until all or nearly all the light is removed, leaving darkness.

The polarizing material allows light waves to be transmitted primarily along only one axis of the transverse waves. If a second polarizing film is added and lined up the same way

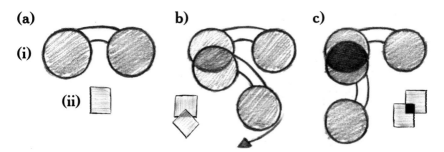

Figure 38.

a) Light intensity is diminished as light passes through polarizing sunglasses (i) or film (ii). b) Place a second sunglass lens on the first one or a second film on the first. Arrange them so that light passes through the lenses or films. When the light intensity is at maximum, the polarizing axes in the two polarizers are parallel. Slowly rotate the second lens or film until c) the polarizing axes are perpendicular (crossed). At this point, all or most of the light is blocked.

(Figure 38a), both will transmit light along matching transverse axes. If the second film or lens is slowly turned so that the axes are not lined up (Figure 38b), very little, if any, light will pass through them (Figure 38c).

The polarization of light is similar to waves on a rope moving into two slotted boards. If the slots are parallel, waves oriented along the direction of the slots will be transmitted. If the slots are perpendicular to each other, no transverse waves can pass through the boards (see Figures 39a and 39b).

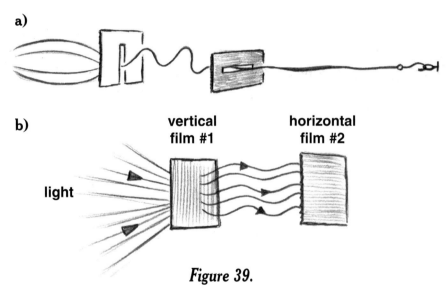

Figure 39.

a) **The behavior of light passing through polarizing films with crossed axes is similar to waves on a rope passing through slotted boards. Transverse waves on a rope are polarized by a vertical slot. The remaining polarized wave is removed by a horizontal slot.**

b) **Nonpolarized light is polarized by polarizing film #1. Remaining polarized light is blocked by polarizing film #2.**

Science Project Ideas

- Repeat Experiment 7.2. Turn the polarizing sunglasses or films so that all or most of the light is blocked. Then rotate a third polarizing film or lens in front of and then behind the other two. Do you observe any change? Next, place the third polarizer between the other two. Slowly rotate the middle lens or film. Do you observe any change? How can you explain what you observe?

- Investigate how honeybees use polarized light to locate and communicate the direction to a source of nectar.

Experiment 7.3

Polarizing Light by Reflection

Materials

- ✓ sheet of glass
- ✓ black construction paper
- ✓ tape
- ✓ protractor
- ✓ cardboard
- ✓ pin
- ✓ paper clip
- ✓ thread
- ✓ flashlight with a good parallel beam

- ✓ a partner
- ✓ 2 pairs of polarizing sunglasses or 2 sheets of polarizing film
- ✓ dark room
- ✓ baking dish
- ✓ water
- ✓ sheet of shiny metal

Is reflected light polarized? To find out, place a sheet of glass on a piece of black paper. Attach a protractor to a flashlight as shown in Figure 40a. Ask a partner to shine the flashlight onto the glass. Look at the reflected beam through a polarizing lens or film. Rotate the lens or film. Does the light intensity change as you rotate the polarizing lens or film? Does the reflected beam appear to be partially polarized?

Ask your partner to shine the light onto the glass at different angles of incidence (see Figure 40b) while you examine the reflected light at a corresponding angle of reflection. At what

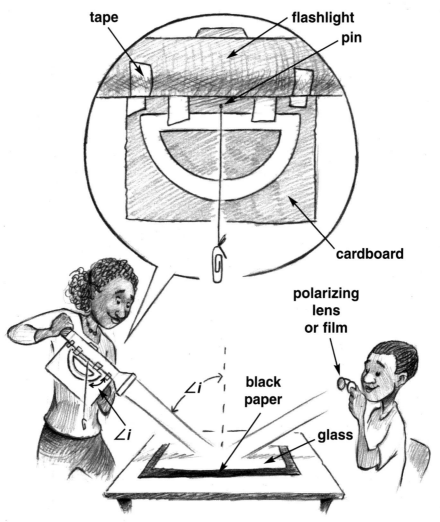

Figure 40.

a) Tape a protractor to a sheet of cardboard. Add a pin at the
   midpoint of the protractor's base. Suspend a paper clip on
   a thread from the pin so that angles of incidence can be
   measured.

b) Shine the light on the glass. Examine the reflected light
   with a polarizing lens or film.

angle of incidence ($\angle i$) is the reflected light of minimum intensity?

Repeat the experiment, but this time use water to reflect the light. First, line a baking dish with black construction paper. Then pour water onto the paper. Is there an angle of incidence at which the reflected light is of minimum intensity? If so, what is the angle? Is it the same angle as it was for glass?

Repeat the experiment once more using a shiny metal surface to reflect the light. Is there an angle of incidence at which the reflected light is of minimum intensity?

Science Project Ideas

- In 1811, Sir David Brewster made an important discovery while experimenting with polarized light. Can you duplicate his experiment?

- Erasmus Bartholin made an important discovery about light refraction while experimenting with calcite (Iceland spar). Can you duplicate his experiment? How is his discovery related to polarized light?

WHAT IS LIGHT?

The experiments you have done strongly suggest that light behaves like waves. It is true that in many circumstances light does behave as if it were waves. Reflection, refraction, diffraction, interference, and polarization can all be explained by assuming that light behaves like waves. However, there are instances in which the behavior of light cannot be explained by a wave model.

When you enter a supermarket, the doors open automatically. These doors are controlled by photoelectric cells. In 1888, Heinrich Hertz, a German physicist, discovered that the charges on negatively charged metal plates could be quickly removed (discharged) by shining light on them. This transfer of light energy to charged particles became known as the photoelectric effect.

Scientists tried to explain the photoelectric effect using a wave model of light. They knew that it would require a significant amount of time before enough wave energy would accumulate to discharge a metal plate. In dim light, hours would pass before any charges would be released—according to a wave model. Yet the photoelectric effect was immediate. As soon as even dim light fell on the charged metal, the metal began to discharge. Clearly, something was wrong with the wave model of light.

In 1905, Albert Einstein explained the photoelectric effect by assuming that light consists of tiny bundles of energy called photons ("particles" of energy). If light energy consists of photons, a single photon may have enough energy to discharge an atom.

The photon (particle) model of light can explain the photoelectric effect and many other phenomena that a wave model cannot. Both waves and photons are used to explain the behavior of light. Neither, alone, can explain all the properties of light: Both have their limitations, both are needed.

LIGHT AND SOUND

We are sure that sound consists of longitudinal waves that travel through air and other substances. We are certain, too, that matter is needed to transmit sound. Sound cannot travel through empty space.

At room temperature, sound waves travel through air at a speed of 330 m/s (1,083 ft/s). They travel faster in solids, liquids, and gases lighter than air. The velocity of sound decreases slightly as the temperature falls and increases slightly with a rise in temperature.

Unlike sound, light can travel through empty space, as well as through transparent forms of matter such as air, glass, and water. The speed of light in a vacuum is very nearly 300,000 km/s (186,000 mi/s) and only slightly less through a gas. In transparent solids and liquids, such as glass and water, the speed of light is less, but still huge compared to the speed of sound.

Appendix

SCIENCE SUPPLY COMPANIES

Carolina Biological Supply Company
2700 York Road
Burlington, NC 27215-3398
(800) 334-5551
http://www.carolina.com

Connecticut Valley Biological
Supply Company
82 Valley Road
P.O. Box 326
Southampton, MA 01073
(800) 628-7748
http://www.ctvalleybio.com

Delta Education
80 Northwest Boulevard
P.O. Box 3000
Nashua, NH 03061-3000
(800) 442-5444
http://www.delta-education.com

Edmund Scientifics
60 Pearce Avenue
Tonawanda, NY 14150-6711
(800) 728-6999
http://scientificsonline.com

Educational Innovations, Inc.
362 Main Avenue
Norwalk, CT 06851
(888) 912-7474
http://www.teachersource.com

Fisher Science Education
4500 Turnberry Drive
Hanover Park, IL 60133
(800) 955-1177
http://www.fisheredu.com

Frey Scientific
100 Paragon Parkway
Mansfield, OH 44903
(800) 225-3739
http://www.freyscientific.com

NASCO-Fort Atkinson
901 Janesville Avenue
P.O. Box 901
Fort Atkinson, WI 53538-0901
(800) 558-9595
http://www.nascofa.com

NASCO-Modesto
4825 Stoddard Road
P.O. Box 3837
Modesto, CA 95352-3837
(800) 558-9595
http://www.nascfao.com

Sargent-Welch/VWR Scientific
P.O. Box 5229
Buffalo Grove, IL 60089-5229
(800) 727-4386
http://www.sargentwelch.com

Science Kit & Boreal Laboratories
777 East Park Drive
P.O. Box 5003
Tonawanda, NY 14150
(800) 828-7777
http://sciencekit.com

Ward's Natural Science
P.O. Box 92912
Rochester, NY 14692-9012
(800) 962-2660
http://www.wardsci.com

Further Reading

BOOKS

Adams, Richard, and Robert Gardner. *Ideas for Science Projects, Revised Edition.* Danbury, Conn.: Watts, 1997.

Bochinski, Julianne Blair. *The Complete Handbook of Science Fair Projects.* New York: Wiley, 1996.

Bombaugh, Ruth. *Science Fair Success, Revised and Expanded.* Springfield, N.J.: Enslow Publishers, Inc., 1999.

Fleisher, Paul. *Waves: Principles of Light, Electricity, and Magnetism.* Minneapolis, Minn.: Lerner Publishing Group, 2001.

Friedhoffer, Robert. *Physics Lab in a Hardware Store.* Danbury, Conn.: Franklin Watts, 1997.

Garner, Robert. *Science Projects About Methods of Measuring.* Berkeley Heights, N.J.: Enslow Publishers, Inc., 2000.

———. *Science Projects About Sound.* Berkeley Heights, N.J.: Enslow Publishers, Inc., 2000.

———. *Science Fair Projects: Planning, Presenting, Succeeding.* Springfield, N.J.: Enslow Publishers, Inc., 1998.

Parker, Steve. *Light and Sound.* Orlando, Fla.: Raintree Steck-Vaughn, 2000.

Tocci, Salvatore. *How to Do a Science Fair Project, Revised Edition.* Danbury, Conn.: Franklin Watts, 1997.

Internet Addresses

Boston Museum of Science
http://www.mos.org/sln/Leonardo/InventorsWorkshop.html

The Exploratorium
http://www.exploratorium.edu

The Franklin Institute Online
http://www.fi.edu

Index